HISTORICAL ESSAYS

HISTORICAL ESSAYS

BY THE LATE

J. B. LIGHTFOOT, D.D., D.C.L., LL.D.

LORD BISHOP OF DURHAM

PUBLISHED BY THE TRUSTEES OF THE LIGHTFOOT FUND

Eugene, Oregon

Wipf and Stock Publishers
199 W 8th Ave, Suite 3
Eugene, OR 97401

Historical Essays
By Lightfoot, J. B.
ISBN: 1-59752-645-2
Publication date 4/14/2006
Previously published by Macmillan and Co., 1895

PREFATORY NOTE

THE Lectures included in this volume were written at different times before Bishop Lightfoot was called to the See of Durham; and they present his character and reading under a somewhat different aspect from that which is shown in his writings that have been already published.

The Lectures on "Christian Life in the Second and Third Centuries" were delivered in St. Paul's Cathedral on the 19th and 26th November and 3rd December 1872. The Lectures on "England during the Latter Half of the Thirteenth Century," based on earlier papers, were delivered before the Philosophical Institution in Edinburgh in February 1874. The General Election filled the newspapers at the time, and not much notice was taken of them. The Lecture on "Donne" formed one of a course of lectures delivered in St. James's Church, Westminster, in 1877, on "the Classic Preachers of the English

Church." The fragment on "The Chapel of St. Peter and the Manor-House of Auckland" was written at the close of the Bishop's life; and volumes of the publications of the Surtees Society, which are in the Library of the Castle, witness to the interest and zeal with which he investigated the history of the building which he adorned with splendid munificence.

Later discoveries have in parts modified the opinions which are expressed in the Lectures; but it has seemed best to leave them just as they were written. Their charm and value lie in the life and warmth with which a master in historical art has sketched some characteristics of the two periods in which lie the roots of our Christian life and of our national life.

The unfinished Essay on "Auckland Castle," while it establishes beyond doubt the nature and extent of Bishop Cosin's work and the original use of the present chapel, does not touch on the difficult and complicated problem of the date of the arcade and other early fragments which it includes. But though incomplete, the Essay is a remarkable example of the enthusiasm with which the Bishop threw himself into inquiries, foreign to the general line of his studies, which were suggested by the circumstances of his life. He gave himself without reserve to all that fell within the range of his immediate duties.

In this lay the secret of his strength and of his happiness. It was a kind of martyrdom to him to leave Cambridge; but when the change was once made, Cambridge was forgotten in the wider activities of Durham.

The Trustees owe their heartiest thanks to the Bishop of Adelaide (Dr. Harmer) for preparing the Lectures for the Press, and to the Master of University College, Durham (Dr. Plummer), for completing the work which Dr. Harmer was obliged to leave unfinished.

B. F. D.

AUCKLAND CASTLE,
    12th July 1895.

EXTRACT FROM THE LAST WILL AND TESTAMENT OF THE LATE JOSEPH BARBER LIGHTFOOT, LORD BISHOP OF DURHAM.

"I BEQUEATH all my personal Estate not hereinbefore
"otherwise disposed of unto [my Executors] upon trust to
"pay and transfer the same unto the Trustees appointed
"by me under and by virtue of a certain Indenture of
"Settlement creating a Trust to be known by the name
"of 'The Lightfoot Fund for the Diocese of Durham'
"and bearing even date herewith but executed by me
"immediately before this my Will to be administered
"and dealt with by them upon the trusts for the pur-
"poses and in the manner prescribed by such Indenture
"of Settlement."

EXTRACT FROM THE INDENTURE OF SETTLEMENT OF "THE LIGHTFOOT FUND FOR THE DIOCESE OF DURHAM."

"WHEREAS the Bishop is the Author of and is
"absolutely entitled to the Copyright in the several
"Works mentioned in the Schedule hereto, and for the

"purposes of these presents he has assigned or intends
"forthwith to assign the Copyright in all the said Works
"to the Trustees. Now the Bishop doth hereby declare
"and it is hereby agreed as follows:—

"The Trustees (which term shall hereinafter be taken
"to include the Trustees for the time being of these
"presents) shall stand possessed of the said Works and of
"the Copyright therein respectively upon the trusts
"following (that is to say) upon trust to receive all
"moneys to arise from sales or otherwise from the said
"Works, and at their discretion from time to time to
"bring out new editions of the same Works or any of
"them, or to sell the copyright in the same or any of
"them, or otherwise to deal with the same respectively,
"it being the intention of these presents that the Trustees
"shall have and may exercise all such rights and powers
"in respect of the said Works and the copyright therein
"respectively, as they could or might have or exercise in
"relation thereto if they were the absolute beneficial
"owners thereof. . . .

"The Trustees shall from time to time, at such
"discretion as aforesaid, pay and apply the income of the
"Trust funds for or towards the erecting, rebuilding,
"repairing, purchasing, endowing, supporting, or providing
"for any Churches, Chapels, Schools, Parsonages, and
"Stipends for Clergy, and other Spiritual Agents in
"connection with the Church of England and within the
"Diocese of Durham, and also for or towards such other
"purposes in connection with the said Church of England,
"and within the said Diocese, as the Trustees may in
"their absolute discretion think fit, provided always that
"any payment for erecting any building, or in relation to

"any other works in connection with real estate, shall be
"exercised with due regard to the Law of Mortmain ; it
"being declared that nothing herein shall be construed as
"intended to authorise any act contrary to any Statute or
"other Law. . . .

"In case the Bishop shall at any time assign to the
"Trustees any Works hereafter to be written or published
"by him, or any Copyrights, or any other property, such
"transfer shall be held to be made for the purposes of
"this Trust, and all the provisions of this Deed shall
"apply to such property, subject nevertheless to any
"direction concerning the same which the Bishop may
"make in writing at the time of such transfer, and in
"case the Bishop shall at any time pay any money, or
"transfer any security, stock, or other like property to
"the Trustees, the same shall in like manner be held for
"the purposes of this Trust, subject to any such contem-
"poraneous direction as aforesaid, and any security, stock
"or property so transferred, being of a nature which can
"lawfully be held by the Trustees for the purposes of
"these presents, may be retained by the Trustees, although
"the same may not be one of the securities hereinafter
"authorised.

"The Bishop of Durham and the Archdeacons of
"Durham and Auckland for the time being shall be
"*ex-officio* Trustees, and accordingly the Bishop and
"Archdeacons, parties hereto, and the succeeding Bishops
"and Archdeacons, shall cease to be Trustees on ceasing
"to hold their respective offices, and the number of the
"other Trustees may be increased, and the power of
"appointing Trustees in the place of Trustees other than
"official Trustees, and of appointing extra Trustees, shall

"be exercised by Deed by the Trustees for the time being, provided always that the number shall not at any time be less than five.

"The Trust premises shall be known by the name of "'The Lightfoot Fund for the Diocese of Durham.'"

CONTENTS

	PAGES
1. CHRISTIAN LIFE IN THE SECOND AND THIRD CENTURIES	1-71
2. COMPARATIVE PROGRESS OF ANCIENT AND MODERN MISSIONS	71-92
3. ENGLAND DURING THE LATTER HALF OF THE THIRTEENTH CENTURY	93-181
4. THE CHAPEL OF ST. PETER AND THE MANOR-HOUSE OF AUCKLAND	182-220
5. DONNE, THE POET-PREACHER	221-245

CHRISTIAN LIFE IN THE SECOND AND THIRD CENTURIES

I

ON the last three Tuesdays your attention has been directed mainly to the social conditions of present and recent ages. I must ask you now to transfer yourselves in imagination to a period dating sixteen or seventeen centuries back. I offer no apology for thus suddenly shifting the scene. While it is necessary to face the problems of the present, it is not less important to review the experiences of the past. If we can only read them aright, the records of the difficulties, the sufferings, the triumphs of early Christianity are replete with lessons of immediate interest. And in some respects the past may claim a preference over the present. The study of contemporary religion and politics will always exercise the most powerful fascination over our minds; but it is beset with the most serious disadvantages. In the first place, we approach the subject with the blind partiality of men who have taken a distinct side in the conflicts which they are reviewing. In the next, as we are placed in the very midst of the events, our point of view is necessarily confused, and we are incapacitated from estimating correctly their proportions. The individual soldier, who is fighting for his life amid the roar of guns and the flashing of steel, is the last man to give a faithful account of the dispositions and the manœuvres by which the victory is lost or won. Only when we take up a position aloof from the field of action can we duly appreciate the relations of all the parts in the great battles of history.

In the three lectures which are allotted to me, I purpose dwelling on some aspects of Christian life in the second and third centuries of our era. For the most part my illustrations will be drawn from the period of the hundred and fifty years which followed upon the close of the first century. My starting-point, therefore, will be marked in secular history by the accession of the Emperor Trajan, and in ecclesiastical history by the death of the last surviving apostle, St. John; for the two events were nearly coincident. My reason for confining myself to these limits is this. I am anxious to exhibit Christianity as an independent force, working in and by itself, without the aid of any extraneous supports or any peculiar advantages. Thus I exclude, on the one hand, the ages when the special influence and extraordinary inspiration of the Apostles might be thought to exempt the Church from the common experiences of history. And on the other hand, I stop short of the time when, under Constantine, the Church entered into an alliance with the State, and it becomes difficult henceforth to estimate how far its triumphs should be ascribed to its own inherent power, and how far to the support of the civil arm. During the period to which I restrict myself, there is no disturbing element in the calculation. Whatever successes it achieved were due solely to its own vital energy, *i.e.* to the working of Christian ideas through the Christian society.

And I do not know how I could better strike the keynote to our investigation than by quoting, at the outset, a remarkable description of the early Christians by one of themselves, who appears to have lived close upon the confines of the Apostolic age. The writing from which the extract is taken—the Epistle to Diognetus—is a fragment without a name and without a date, a single page torn out of the vast volume of Christian literature in the second century, which, with a few meagre exceptions, has altogether perished: a mere scrap saved from the ravages of time, like one of those fabled Sibylline leaves, borne fluttering on the winds, coming to us we know not whence, but traced in characters instinct with an energy and a life which is not of the earth.

"Christians," says this anonymous writer, "are not distinguished from the rest of mankind either in territory or in speech or in habits of life. For they neither dwell in cities of their own, nor use any different language, nor practise any strange fashions. But, while they dwell in cities either Greek or barbarian, according to the lot of each man, and observe the local customs in their dress and their food and all their ordinary habits, yet in their own mode of life they exhibit a conception which is marvellous and confessedly unique. They dwell each in his own country, but they dwell there as sojourners. They share every duty as citizens, and they suffer every indignity as foreigners. Every foreign country is a fatherland to them; and every fatherland is foreign to them. They marry, like all men; they beget children, but they do not destroy their offspring. They spread a common table, which yet is not common. They are in the flesh, but they do not live after the flesh. They pass their days on earth, but they have their citizenship in heaven. They obey the established laws, and they surpass the laws in their lives. They love all men, and they are persecuted by all. They are unknown, and yet they are condemned. They are put to death, and yet they are made alive. They are paupers, and they make many rich; they lack all things, and they abound in all things; they are dishonoured, and they are glorified in their dishonour; they are calumniated, and they are justified; they are reviled, and they bless; they are insulted, and they respect. Doing good, they are punished as evil-doers; punished, they rejoice as being made alive. By Jews they are assaulted as foreigners; and by Gentiles they are persecuted; and their haters cannot assign the cause of their enmity. In one word—what the soul is in the body, this Christians are in the world. The soul is dispersed through all the members of the body; and Christians throughout the cities of the world. The soul dwells in the body, but is not of the body; so Christians dwell in the world, and are not of the world. The soul, being invisible, is imprisoned in the body, which is visible. So Christians are perceived to be in the world, but their piety remains invisible. The flesh hates the soul and wars against it, though it suffers no wrong, because it is prevented from enjoying pleasures. So the world hates Christians, though suffering no wrong, because they are opposed to pleasures. The soul loves the flesh and the members which hate it. So Christians love those that hate them. The soul is enclosed in the body, and yet itself sustains the body. So Christians are shut up in the world as in a prison-house, and yet they themselves sustain the world. The soul being immortal dwells in a mortal tabernacle. So Christians sojourn among corruptible things, while they await the incorruption that is in heaven. The soul, by hard fare in meat and drink, becomes better. So Christians, when punished, increase more and more from day to day, so noble is the post which God has assigned to them, and which it is not lawful for them to decline. For, as I said, this is no earthly invention which has been delivered to them, nor is it a plan of human devising which they hold it a duty to guard thus carefully. But in very truth God Himself, the Almighty and All-creative and Invisible, God Himself from heaven planted among men the Truth, and the holy and incomprehensible Word, and established Him in their hearts: not sending to men, as one might imagine, some inferior officer or angel or ruler, or one of those beings who have the guidance of things terrestrial, or of those to whom is committed the administration of the heavens, but the very Artificer and Creator of the Universe, by whom He made the heavens, by whom He enclosed the sea within its proper bounds, whose mysterious ordinances all the celestial bodies faithfully obey. . . . Did He send Him, as any *man* might conceive, to establish a tyranny, or to inspire fear and alarm? Nay, not so, but in gentleness and meekness. He sent Him as a king sending his son, a king. He sent Him as being God; He sent Him as to men; He sent Him, as saving, as persuading, not as compelling: for compulsion has no place with God. He sent Him, as inviting, not as persecuting; He sent Him in love and not in judgment. For He *will* send Him in judgment, and who shall abide His presence? Seest thou not how His servants are thrown to wild beasts, that they may deny their Master, and yet do not succumb? Seest thou not, that the greater the number of those punished, the more does the number of the others increase? These things are not like the works of man: they are the power of God; they are tokens of His presence."

I do not know what impression this passage may have made on my hearers; but to myself it seems to embody the very spirit of the Gospel. In its thrilling earnestness and its lofty simplicity, its undaunted courage and its unbounded hope, it presents to us the liveliest picture of the struggles and the aspirations and the victories of Christianity in the early ages. Compare it, if you will, with the noblest utterances of heathen sage or moralist of the time, with the righteous dogmatism of an Epictetus or the plaintive aspirations of a M. Aurelius; you will see at once that it soars into a loftier region than any of these. There is an energy and a vitality in it, a consciousness of strength, a capacity of endurance, and an assurance of triumph, which is wholly different in kind from the religious sentiments of heathendom. And if you ask an explanation of the difference, if you probe the secret of this novel force, you will find the solution to be very simple. The writer himself leaves you in no doubt about this. He does not refer you to the moral precepts of the Gospel, or to the social organization of the Church, or to the philosophical dogmas of Christianity, but to a Person and a Fact. Not a word is said about any of those five causes which Gibbon parades before his readers when he attempts to account for the unparalleled triumphs of Christianity—the pertinacious zeal of the Christians, and the alluring promises of future bliss, and the miraculous powers claimed by the primitive Church, and the austere morality of the new society, and the efficient discipline of the body. These, so far as they are causes, are only secondary causes; they are not the root and stem, but only the leaves and fruit of the great tree which was to overshadow the earth. The root itself, as this writer conceives it, is the incarnation of the Divine Word, the realization of God's love and God's presence through the human life and death of Christ. Here is the mainspring of this unique energy, the hidden source of this new and vigorous life.

And the life itself? In a few simple and bold touches it is described to us. The description consists of a series of contrasts arising out of the fundamental position of the Christian. The Christian inhabits two worlds, lives two lives. To each of these he has direct obligations. These spheres, however, are not distinct and apart, but constantly intersect and overlap each other; and the great problem which must engage the attention of every conscientious man is how he can harmonize these claims. The conditions of the problem will differ in various states of society; but in some form or other it must always press for solution. It is as fresh to you and to me to-day as it was to any member of this small and persecuted sect more than seventeen centuries ago. But to the early Christian the problem was beset with the most cruel perplexities, from which we happily are free. At every turn the question presented itself, "How am I at once to render to Cæsar the things which are Cæsar's, and to God the things which are God's?" and he must be ready with an immediate practical answer. How he solved the problem it will be my business to show in these lectures.

Keeping this object therefore in view, I think that the history of Christian life in the early centuries may be conveniently treated under three heads. In the time which remains to me this evening, I shall speak of the relations of the Christian to society. Next Tuesday I hope to discuss with you his position as regards the law and the government, or (in modern phrase) the relations of Church and State. And in my third and last lecture, I intend to say something about Christian worship in these primitive times. The first subject has no fixed centre about which it will revolve. The interest of the second will gather about the martyrdoms. The third will be more or less localized in the catacombs.

Following out this plan, and treating this evening of the Christian in relation to society, I shall confine myself to three points, which will be sufficient to occupy my time—the social position, the social difficulties, and the social triumphs of the early Christians.

1. It was a constant taunt of the early antagonists of Christianity, that the new religion did not recruit its ranks from the most exalted or the most intellectual or the most respectable classes of society.

The philosopher Celsus, who appears to have written about the middle of the second century, makes it a matter of reproach that the active members of the sect were wool-workers and cobblers and curriers, the most ignorant and boorish of mankind, who were marvellously eloquent in a knot of women or boys or slaves, but had not a word to say for themselves when confronted with sensible men.

The taunt was an old foe with a new face. Long ago the question had been asked, as if the mere asking were sufficient to bar all further inquiry, "Have any of the rulers or of the Pharisees believed?" And now the language of the Jewish priests is unconsciously echoed by the Gentile sophists: "Have any of the princes, any of the senators, any of the philosophers believed?"

There was just enough foundation, in fact, for this taunt to arm it with a sting. It might not be so true now as it had been a century before, when St. Paul uttered the words that there were not many wise after the flesh, not many powerful, not many noble, either among the teachers or among the disciples of the new sect; yet still its converts would be drawn mainly from the less influential and the less educated classes of society. But what then? Was there any ground for assuming that either wealth or rank or education was a necessary condition of estimating correctly the claims of a religion which professed to disregard all conventional distinctions, and to address itself to man as man?

This was not the first time, and it certainly will not have been the last, when the noblest and truest impulses, whether religious or moral, have worked upward from beneath. There was nothing in the social experiences of the high-born and wealthy, or in the technical education of the philosopher or the rhetorician, which peculiarly qualified them for appraising the worth of Christianity. Nay, just so far as the higher classes were removed from the hardest trials of their fellow-men, just so far as convention had chilled and stiffened in them the common instincts of humanity, they were absolutely incapacitated as judges. To mankind at large, with its sorrows and its sufferings, with its consciousness of sin and its aspirations after good, the Gospel message was addressed; and from them it found a ready response.

But, indeed, this was a dangerous weapon for the adversaries of Christianity to wield. It was wrested from their hands and turned with deadly effect against themselves. It had been the proudest achievement of Socrates that he brought down philosophy from the skies to the level of common life. But the Gospel achieved a far greater triumph. "Every Christian mechanic," said Tertullian triumphantly, "has found out God, and can show Him to others"; though Plato said that it was difficult to discover Him, and next to impossible to communicate the discovery when made. This father contemptuously rejects what he calls the illusions of civilization. He turns aside from the training of the schools, and he addresses himself to the primary, unsophisticated, unencrusted consciousness of man: "I summon thee, O Soul, simple and rude and unpolished and unlearned, such as they possess thee who possess thee by thyself, the very real soul in its integrity—from the roadside, from the thoroughfare, from the weaver's shop. I want thine inexperience, since thy poor experience is trusted by none. I ask for just what thou bringest to man, just what thoughts thou hast learnt either from thyself or from thy Creator." "We do not talk great things," wrote Cyprian, "but we live them."

But in fact the allegation of Celsus was not true. If rank and knowledge did not form any special qualification for the acceptance of the Gospel, they did not interpose any serious barrier. Already, when Celsus wrote, the tide was rising, and it became evident that even the highest eminences of intellectual and social life must soon be flooded. Even in the earlier years of the Apostolic age the conversion of a Roman proconsul, Sergius Paulus, was an augury of ultimate victory. Before the first century had run out, a prince and princess of the reigning house, Clemens and Domitilla, the cousins of the Emperor Domitian, suffered for their adherence to the new faith. Soon after, about the year 110, Pliny reports to the Emperor that many "of *every* rank" were infected with the strange superstition. In the latter half of the second century Irenæus speaks more than once of Christians at the

Imperial Court. At the close of the century Marcia, who was all-powerful with the worthless Commodus, seems to have been herself a Christian, and certainly extorted from him many concessions in their favour. About this time Tertullian, writing at Carthage, avows that Christianity had invaded every class of society, and that even official dignity was passing over to its ranks. And twenty or thirty years later, the Emperor Alexander Severus, if not himself a Christian, at least acted with friendly partiality towards the growing sect, while his mother corresponded with the greatest Christian teacher of the day.

Nor was it otherwise with intellectual culture. Already, when Celsus wrote, Christianity was receiving constant recruits from the ranks of philosophy. The Platonist Justin and the Stoic Pantænus, dissatisfied with the hollow professions of their respective sects, had sought and had found in the Gospel satisfaction for their deepest wants. Advance another half-century and the victory is unmistakable. With all his faults of taste and style, Tertullian stands out pre-eminent as the literary genius of his age. His fiery eloquence and his vivid imagination have no rival among his classical contemporaries. After all allowance made for his allegorical subtleties, Origen far outstrips the heathen thinkers of his time. We cannot name any classical author of that age who combines in the same degree the profound insight of the philosopher with the patience and the acumen of the critic.

But, not content with attacking the intellectual capacity and social rank of the Christian converts, Celsus did not spare even their moral antecedents. He urged that others who invited worshippers to initiation in their mysteries, strictly confined their invitation to those who were "clean of hand and wise of speech," who were "pure from all contamination, and whose soul was conscious of no evil, who had lived a good and upright life." On the other hand, the summons of the Christian was the very reverse of all this: "Whosoever is a sinner, whosoever is foolish, whosoever is a little child, (in one word) whosoever is a miserable wretch, he shall be received into the kingdom of heaven." "Whom do you mean," he asked, "by the sinner? Why, of course, the dishonest and the thief and the burglar and the poisoner, and the robber of temples and the violater of graves."

This was especially dangerous ground for the assailant of Christianity to occupy. While making the attack he had exposed his own flank, and the opportunity was not lost by the defenders. Wholly unconscious what an advantage he was giving them, he avowed the utter impotence of religion to effect any great moral reformation in a man, and he urged that it was next to impossible to change the character of one who was habituated to evil; and on this ground he objected to the Founder of Christianity that he came to "save sinners," when he ought to have addressed himself to just men. The answer was triumphant. The Christian Apologist could point to hundreds and thousands of men who had been reclaimed from the worst vices by the Gospel, and were now living pure and honest and peaceful and self-denying lives. The bitterest taunt of the assailant was the grandest boast of the Apologist. If, on the other hand, the religion of Celsus could effect no moral reformation, that religion stood self-condemned.

2. But whatever might be his condition in life, the Christian found his path *beset* with practical difficulties. These would doubtless be greater in the higher ranks, and greatest of all in official circles; but the humblest Christian was confronted by them in almost every action of life. It is next to impossible for us to realize the *ubiquity*, the *obtrusiveness*, the *intrusiveness* of polytheism. A spiritual religion from its very nature does not force itself on observation in the same way. Just because it addressed itself to the outward senses, polytheism could not be evaded. All the public offices at Rome were connected with the sanctuary of some god. The temple of Mars was the war office; the temple of Juno, the mint; the temple of Saturn, the treasury; and so forth. Thus every official duty was bound up with some religious sanction. All commercial transactions, again, were represented by their appropriate deity. At the same time, when Roman civilization and enlightenment had reached their highest pitch during the reign of Augustus, the importation of

corn from Egypt, on which the Roman populace largely depended for support, was deified, and a niche assigned to the new goddess Annona in the pantheon of Roman worship. This is very much as though, among ourselves, Free-trade were to receive the honours of an apotheosis. But the elasticity of polytheism was not confined to matters of general and public interest. Each several locality had its patron deity—the house and the field, the stable and the farmyard. Every sanitary regulation—even the sewage of Rome—was under the protection of some god. Every desire and every sentiment, every virtue—one might almost say, every vice—of man, underwent an apotheosis. Nay, so far did this passion for deification go, that there was hardly a ramification of human life, and hardly a development of human action, which was left unoccupied. With savage humour Tertullian parades the names of gods and goddesses who presided over the birth and nurture of a child—Edulia and Potina over its eating and drinking, Cunina over its slumbers in the cradle, Rumina over its suckling, Farinus or Locutius over its first lessons in talking, Statina over its first efforts at standing, with numberless others. Amidst this multitudinous throng of deities, the position of the early converts must have been difficult indeed. To keep themselves pure from idols, as it was their most elementary duty, so also was their direst perplexity. No wonder that to the careless heathen they appeared morose, reserved, unsympathetic, in private life.

How could they do otherwise than abstain in great measure from the commonest interests of their heathen neighbours? No wonder that as citizens they were charged with want of patriotism. The affairs of state were too intimately bound up with the recognition of polytheism to leave them free.

The charge brought by the heathen historian against Flavius Clemens, whom I have already mentioned, is, that he was a man of contemptible indolence. His indolence was doubtless enforced. His principles left him no choice. In many provinces of public life it was impossible for a man to engage without entangling himself in the meshes of idolatry. Hence it is a common accusation against the early Christians that they were idle and unprofitable in public affairs. The Emperor would be left without an army, urged Celsus, if all men thought with the Christians. This was a gross exaggeration. "How can this be," replied Tertullian, "with men living among you, having the same food, the same dress, the same appliances, the same necessities of life? With you we inhabit this world with its market-places, its shambles, its baths, its inns, its workshops, its fairs, its other places of common resort. With you *we* likewise engage in navigation, in war, in agriculture; we mix in commerce and in art like yourselves; we contribute our labour to your common good." In vain the Christian apologists urged these patent facts; in vain they contended that, though in some respects the State might be the loser, yet it was more than compensated by their honesty, their sobriety, their orderliness, their benevolence. The charge was not altogether unfounded. There are epochs when even the obligations of patriotism must yield to the imperious claims of a higher duty; when the regeneration of society demands the sacrifice of every individual and local interest, of country, of home, of self, to its own paramount needs. At such a crisis the dislocation of all social and political relations is inevitable. Then amid the birth-throes of a new order the piercing cry is wrung from humanity in its agony and dismay. The great day has come which was foretold, when there should be "distress of nations with perplexity, men's hearts failing them for fear." But then also the hope, the deliverance, the light, is at hand. Men are bidden to look up and to lift up their heads, for their "redemption draweth nigh."

And not less perplexing was the position of the Christian with regard to common duties and interests of life. Look for a moment at the ordinary amusements of heathen society. It was a matter of common observation that the Roman people, besides their bread, cared for nothing but the public games. But the conscientious Christian was absolutely forbidden to take any part in these degrading spectacles. To say nothing of the religious character which attached to them, their moral aspect was revolting to the Christian mind. In our own age we hold it a disgrace to our common Christianity that one relic of these demoralizing spectacles should still linger in a European country—the bull-fights of Spain, the legacy of the Moorish occupation. But compare these with the bloody scenes of the Roman amphitheatre, and they pale into insignificance. The slaughter of a few bulls and a few horses now and then would have seemed tame and spiritless to a Roman sightseer. It has been truly said that the number of wild beasts slaughtered at a single festival in Rome would have more than stocked all the zoological gardens in Europe. When the theatre of Pompeius was dedicated, from 500 to 600 lions were hunted, besides other wild beasts from Africa. At the inauguration of the Colosseum, under the Emperor Titus, it is reported that not less than 9000 animals, wild and tame, were slain.

Nor do these instances stand alone. After all allowance made for possible exaggeration, the slaughter must have been frightful. What then would be the feelings of a Christian at this reckless effusion of blood, this wanton infliction of pain, at which thousands of women and children looked on and applauded? But the darkest tale remains yet to be told. The Roman spectator was not satisfied with the slaughter of animal life. He needed some keener excitement than this. Without human victims the zest of such entertainments would soon be blunted. At the games which Trajan gave after his victories over the Dacians, as many as 10,000 men are said to have fought in the amphitheatre.

During the year of his ædileship the first Gordian exhibited gladiatorial shows every month, sometimes as many as 500 pairs of combatants, never less than 150. On these occasions the floor would be strewn with the bodies of the fallen, "butchered to make a Roman holiday." In the instances given the numbers are doubtless exceptionally large; but on a smaller scale such frightful spectacles were constant. Where pairs of gladiators or troops of combatants failed, the thirst for human blood was allayed (shall we not say was whetted?) by the spectacle of condemned criminals mangled and devoured by lions and tigers in the arena. The details recorded on these occasions are too horrible to repeat. Ask yourselves, then, what sympathy the Christians could have had with the common amusement of their heathen fellow-countrymen— the Christians who would shudder to think that they themselves might be the next victims of this inhuman passion for blood.

But not less in his domestic relations would the perplexities of his position be felt by the Christian. Again and again the demands of polytheism must be confronted and must be denied. Again and again the immoralities of heathendom must be denounced, or at least shunned. Tertullian draws a vivid picture of the difficulties which beset a Christian wife mated to a pagan husband—of the conflict between her duties and his exactions. It is no doubt taken from the life; and such complications must have been frequent. We read of husbands accusing their wives, of masters punishing their slaves, because, having become Christians, they could no longer share in or connive at the impurities and the degradations of their former lives. The time which was predicted had come, when "there should be five in one house divided, three against two, and two against three"; when "they should be betrayed by parents and brethren and kinsfolk and friends"; when "a man's foes should be they of his own household."

3. I have already occupied so much time on the first two points on which I promised to speak, that I shall have to dismiss very briefly the third—the social influence of the Christians. The Divine Founder had declared that His followers were destined to be "the salt of the earth." The author whom I quoted at the outset, as you will remember, puts the same thought in other words. The Christians, he says, are to the world as the soul to the body—the reviving, sustaining, regenerating principle of its moral and social life. I have not time to follow out the thought now; but I confidently appeal to the history of early Christianity in verification of this claim. "Christ appeared," says St. Augustine, "to men in a decrepit and dying world, that, while all around them was decaying, they might through Him receive a new and youthful life." Society, which was worn out and prematurely aged when Augustine wrote, has revived. And to what is this revival

due? To the barbarian races, it may be said, which supplanted the effete Greek and Roman. Yes, to these, as to fresh blood infused into the body; but the inspiring soul, the vital energy, was Christianity.

To substantiate the moral triumphs of early Christianity I might appeal to the testimony both of sincere advocates like Justin, and of calm-judging antagonists like Pliny. But it would be impossible to range over the whole field of moral conduct. I shall therefore single out two points, in which Christianity set itself from the first to work a social reformation, and in which the superiority of Christian over heathen morality is signally vindicated.

The first of these is the respect for human life. If it fell within my limits, I might tell how the butcheries of the amphitheatre, having survived the establishment of Christianity, were finally extinguished by the heroism of a Christian monk. But another example is more directly connected with my subject. You will remember how the writer whom I first quoted claims it as a special honour to the Christians that they did not "destroy their offspring." This incidental notice is a startling revelation of the prevalence of this crime. And it does not stand alone. Seneca, writing to his mother, evidently considers that he is bestowing no common praise on her when he says that she did not, like so many ladies of her rank, destroy the hope of offspring. Life, even inchoate life, *must* be infinitely precious to the Christian; for it contains the germ of an immortal being, the hope of an eternal bliss. To destroy before birth, or to expose after birth—trifling offences, if offences at all to the heathen conscience—became to him a heinous and a deadly sin.

The other point to which I ask your attention before I close is the influence of Christianity on the separation of class from class, more especially on the distinction between the freeman and the slave. Now Christianity did not directly attack social or political institutions. St. Paul directs the slave to acquiesce in his condition, cheered with the thought that, though he is the bondsman of his master, yet he is the freedman of Christ. But at the same time it instilled principles which in the end must prove fatal to such an institution as slavery. It pronounced that in Christ there was no distinction of bond or free. It declared in the broadest terms the universal brotherhood of the faithful. And in her own ecclesiastical arrangements the Church fearlessly carried out this principle. The slave would kneel by his master's side in public prayer, and by his master's side would receive the Eucharistic bread and wine. But she did more than this. She admitted freely to her highest offices those who had risen from the lowest ranks. In the middle of the second century, Hermas, the author of the *Shepherd*, writes as a slave; yet he was brother of Pius, then Bishop of Rome. In the beginning of the third century, again, the bishopric of Rome itself was occupied by Callistus, who had himself been a slave of one Carpophorus, an officer in the imperial household. The consequence was inevitable. If this principle was once admitted in practice, slavery was doomed. The institution might die hard, but die it must. When in all that concerns the highest interests of man the slave was recognized as his master's equal, the conventional outward barrier could not be maintained. Slavery lingered long and struggled hard. It was reserved for our own generation to see the end. But its deathblow was given when St. Paul declared that all men are one in Christ.

I have thus endeavoured, however imperfectly, to set before you the struggles and the triumphs of early Christianity in its relation to society. I would only remind you in conclusion that the lists are not closed, that the fight is not ended, that the victory is not won. The conditions of the contest change from age to age; but the underlying principle is ever the same. You, sirs, are the heirs not only of the lessons, not only of the achievements, but also of the responsibilities and the struggles of the past. If you would prove yourselves worthy of your name and ancestry, if you would appreciate to the full the magnificent possibilities of your calling, you must be animated by the same spirit by which the most splendid victories of the past have been won. You must not forget that, with all the engrossing cares of your earthly avocations, you are yet citizens of a heavenly polity; that, though in the world, you are yet not of the world. You must be strong with the strength of the master-conviction that the work which you are called to do is not a work of human invention; that God has sent upon earth His Eternal Word, to take up His abode in your hearts, and to transform you into His own perfections.

II

ON Tuesday last I reviewed the relations of the Christian to society. This evening I shall discuss his relations to the State. On the former occasion I pointed out how he faced the problems of life: now I shall show how he met the terrors of death.

Living, as we do, in an age when the rights of the individual are loudly proclaimed and scrupulously respected, it is difficult for us to conceive the tyranny which in ancient times the State exercised over the thoughts and the actions of the subject. Not content with levying taxes and enforcing service, with maintaining order and punishing crime, the State *prescribed* to the subject his duties and his amusements, his religion and his mode of life. We talk much, and (though the term is often abused) we talk truly, of the rights of conscience. An ancient politician knew nothing of any such rights. The individual had no claims which were inconvenient to the State, or interfered in any way with its compactness and harmony. He was only a crank or a wheel in the vast machinery; and he must move in regular subordination to the whole. Patriotism was the one paramount virtue. Principles of morality drew their authority and their efficacy from legal codes and political institutions. Conscience and toleration were words unrecognized in the vocabulary of an ancient statesman. Conscience was a possible interference with the demands of patriotism; and toleration was a dangerous encroachment on the stability of public order.

Modern society is separated from ancient society by this vast moral gulf. We regard it as the inalienable right of every man that his opinions and his religion shall be free. It may be necessary to control his actions or even his words, but he is at least allowed to think and to worship as he will. The State exists for the individual, and not the individual for the State.

How largely this change has been brought about by Christianity will be evident at once. Christianity, indeed, protests against the unbridled license and stubborn self-will which seems to be the special danger of our age; for it teaches that the units are related to the whole, as the limbs to the body, each working in subordination to the general health, though each performing its own proper functions. But, on the other hand, Christianity has emphasized the individual man, as he was never emphasized before. This it has done, because it has taught that he is directly and personally responsible to a greater than any earthly power; that all human claims and interests, even the most imposing, must yield to this higher obligation; that he is not a dying atom in a dying universe, a transient phenomenon, a fleeting breath, but a being endowed with an immortal, unquenchable life. Thus his individuality is a power in the economy of the universe, which demands respect; and his conscience is a sanctuary, which cannot be violated without sacrilege.

Now in Rome the ancient idea was pressed with remorseless logic. The magnificent capacities of legislation and government, which distinguished the Roman, tended to the exceptional exaltation of the State at the expense of the individual. Religion itself was cast in a political mould. The worship of the ancient Roman was essentially political, as that of the ancient Greek was artistic. His deities were political powers; his ceremonials political functions. Religion was the mere handmaid of politics. We ourselves can only conceive of theology as in its very nature firm, immutable, absolute. Otherwise it forfeits its claim to the title of theology, because the truth cannot change. This was not the idea of the ancient Roman. His theology avowedly changed with the changing exigencies of the State. It was just as elastic, and just as rigid, as the form of government or the limits of the empire.

1. Thus, for instance, as Rome extended her sway over distant nations, she at the same time enlarged the boundaries of her mythology. With a marvellous power of assimilation she incorporated her conquests; but this incorporation would not be

complete unless the religious arrangements kept pace with the political. Accordingly, it was her policy to recognize the religions of the subject peoples. This recognition was not a mere toleration. It was a direct acknowledgment of their value, in some sense of their truth. Each fresh people whom she conquered had deities of its own. She accepted these deities, gave them a place in her Pantheon, adopted them into her theology. It is difficult for us to conceive a state of mind in which such elasticity of religious worship was possible. In theology we hold that a thing either is or is not, and that no change of circumstance ought to make any difference here, because no change can convert truth into untruth or untruth into truth. But with the polytheist the case was different. When the Roman had conquered a foreign nation, he held that he had conquered its gods also; and he felt no more scruple in conceding to them the honour of adoration than he felt in restoring a province to a defeated prince or extending the franchise to a subject people. In this way, as the Roman Empire advanced, the gods of Egypt, of Syria, of the farther East, found a resting-place in the Pantheon of Rome.

2. And again, when the form of the constitution changed, the theology of the Roman was modified also. I allude to the deification of the Emperor, and I will ask your special attention to this point, not only because it is in itself the most monstrous phenomenon in religious history, but also because it

is the very pivot on which our investigation this evening will turn. At the very moment when the world had reached its highest point of civilization and culture, when political and legislative ability were achieving their most signal triumphs—in an age of remarkable progress and enlightenment which was unequalled in ancient, and has only been equalled quite recently in modern times—this portentous development of polytheism was invented. The apotheosis of a living emperor, indeed, might be somewhat exceptional. It was confined, for the most part, to the provinces, where his worship was the symbol and the acknowledgment of Roman supremacy. Yet monsters like Caligula and Nero claimed and obtained divine honours during their lifetime in Rome itself; and Domitian was wont to be addressed as "my Lord and my God." But the deification of the Emperors after their decease became at length almost a matter of course. "Alas!" said Vespasian, when he felt his fatal illness approaching, "I apprehend I am going to be a god." And thus a single generation saw enrolled among the immortal powers, whom it was required to propitiate with sacrifice and adoration, a brutal sensualist like Commodus and a bloodthirsty fratricide like Caracalla. Nay, to such extremes was the principle carried that any relationship or even connexion with the reigning sovereign might confer the honours of apotheosis. At one time it was a child of four months old, at another a dissolute and effeminate favourite, who was raised to the ranks of the gods. And the world looked on, assented, worshipped, (shall we say?) believed. Here and there a philosopher laughed in his sleeve; but he too accepted the position. One body of men alone held out against this monstrous outrage on common sense and common decency, firm, unflinching, resolute even to death, an insignificant despised sect called Christians. They refused to bow before the hideous idol which Roman statecraft had set up. They held it better to forfeit peace, to forfeit liberty, to forfeit life itself, to be gibbeted on the cross, to be burnt at the stake, to be mangled by wild beasts, than to tell or to act the lie of lies, to put one pinch of incense on the accursed altar, or to offer one word of prayer to the accursed name. In the interests of human progress (I speak not now of divine truth), do they not deserve our undying gratitude?

And yet this monstrous development was the natural, we might almost say the inevitable, consequence of a Roman's conception of religion. On the downfall of the Republic, all the chief offices were concentrated in the person of the Emperor. Tribune, pontiff, imperator, often consul, he was the fountain-head of all civil as well as military power. If not in theory, at least in practice, he *was* the State. Now Roman religion, as we saw, was the mere reflection of Roman politics. It was not, as all true religion must be, a supreme controlling paramount authority, to which individuals and governments alike owe allegiance. In its very nature, therefore, it would perforce adapt itself to the altered circumstances of the time. Concentrated political power demanded a corresponding concentration in the object of religious worship. The person of the Emperor was the obvious response to this demand. The Emperor, therefore, was deified. His divinity was a symbol of the constitution; his worship was a guarantee of loyalty.

How then did these facts affect the position of the Christians? We have seen that there was a singular elasticity in the recognition of foreign religions on the part of the Roman government. It was tolerant, and more than tolerant; it was broad and liberal to an extent which is perfectly astonishing to us. We might, therefore, have presumed that under such a system Christianity would have had the fairest field, and the largest liberty. But a moment's reflection will correct this anticipation. From its very nature Christianity could not expect the toleration which was extended to other religions. Christianity claims to be absolute, paramount, universal. If it is not this, it is nothing at all. It cannot consent to go shares with other systems in the allegiance of its adherents. The God of the Christians will brook no rival. If the Christians had been satisfied with a niche for their Divine Founder in the Roman Pantheon side by side with the deities of Greece or Syria or Egypt, with Cybele and Isis and Astarte, the compromise would have been readily accepted. It is even said that Tiberius proposed to the Senate to recognize our Lord among the adopted gods of Rome. The story may not be true, but it correctly represents the religious sentiment of the Roman people. It is quite certain that at a later date Alexander Severus did place an image of Christ in his private chapel along with the other gods to whom he offered his devotions. Such a compromise the Christian could not accept. Christ must have all, or He will take nothing. The Roman was astonished, perplexed, check-mated, by the attitude which the Christian assumed. It seemed to him so unconciliatory, so exacting, so unreasonable. He could not rise to the conception of an absolute religion, of a supreme and exclusive God. His only idea of a religion was that it was a national religion; of a god, that he was a local god. With such he knew how to deal: but here was a novel phenomenon. Celsus, the antagonist of Christianity, treats it as a ridiculous notion that Greeks and barbarians, Asiatics, Europeans, Africans, should all agree in the same religious worship. He lays it down as an axiom that men are bound to worship the gods after the manner of their country. It is a flagrant crime in his eyes that the Christians have broken loose from the national religion of the Jews. In this he only expresses the prevailing sentiment in ancient Greece and Rome.

Moreover, the idea of a universal exclusive religion, as it was foreign to ancient conceptions, so also was antagonistic to political expediency. The shrewd courtier and statesman Mæcenas is related to have advised the Emperor Augustus, when he assumed the reins of government, " to worship the gods in all respects according to the laws of his country, and to compel others to do the same," adding, that those who introduced new deities would be misled into adopting foreign laws, and that thus secret conspiracies would be fomented. It was a fundamental maxim of ancient legislation, maintained by the wisest philosophers and statesmen, that no man should be allowed to worship any god who had not yet been formally adopted by the law.

And the God of the Christians, from the very nature of the case, could never be so adopted. Hence the large tolerance of the Romans became essentially intolerant where Christianity was concerned. *Non licet esse vos*—" The law gives you no standing-ground ; you are not allowed to exist"— this was the common outcry against the Christians, the legal justification of their persecutors, whenever there was a fresh access of popular fury.

But this was not all. Their own religion was forbidden. Their gatherings were prohibited. If the matter had rested here, their difficulties might have been great, but they would not have been insuperable. By prudent reserve and studious concealment they might perhaps have eluded notice. But the law was not satisfied with these negative demands. The Christians were required to do certain definite overt acts. They were asked to sacrifice to the genius of the living Emperor, to recognize the divinity of the dead Emperor. It was common loyalty to acquiesce; it was sheer treason to decline. Their refusal was a blow aimed at the vitals of the State. If it had been only Neptune or Minerva or Apollo whom they treated with contempt, they might indeed have aroused the indignation of the populace, but they would not have ruffled the equanimity of the government. "You worship Cæsar," writes Tertullian, "with greater awe than Olympian Jove himself." "You would sooner perjure yourselves by all the gods together, than by the genius of Cæsar alone."

I trust I have said enough to explain the momentous character of the conflict. It is quite clear that neither side could yield an inch; that the struggle must be resolute and uncompromising, must be internecine. There was an irreconcilable antagonism between the religious ideas of Christianity and the political institutions of the age. It was the instinct of self-preservation which prompted their heathen rulers to persecute the Christians. A far-sighted statesman might have anticipated that the political fabric would gradually crumble under the touch of the Christian idea. Hence the most cruel persecutors of the Christians were not always the worst rulers or the worst men. We may be startled to find that Christianity suffered more under Marcus Aurelius than under any of the early Emperors. Mr. J.

Stuart Mill regards the attitude of this Emperor towards the Christians as "a tragical fact." It is only tragical in the same sense in which much else connected with this virtuous sovereign is tragical. Is it not an infinitely tragical fact that this same emperor obtained the apotheosis of his profligate wife Faustina, and of his dissolute colleague, L. Verus, building temples for their worship, instituting priesthoods in their names, and in all respects yielding them divine honours? With all his personal amiability and all his philosophical training, he was as much a slave to the system under which he was educated as the most degraded of his predecessors or the most ignorant of his subjects. The deification of imperialism was a primary article of his creed, an absolute necessity of his position. With him it appeared a sufficient claim to divinity in a shameless woman that she was an Emperor's wife, and in a worthless libertine that he was an Emperor's colleague. Humanly speaking, it was impossible for such a man to be a Christian.

Still less could the Christians yield. The war was waged on their side for the most part passively, by careful abstention from politics, by persistent refusal of compromise, by patient endurance under suffering; but their determination was not the less real for this. They felt, for they could not help feeling, the magnitude of the conflict. It might seem a very small thing to throw a few grains of incense on an altar, or to utter a few syllables of adulation to an image; but on that trifling act and those fleeting words hung the most momentous issues which could affect the destiny of mankind. For the alternative offered in the name of religion was simply this: on the one hand, the absolute bondage to a mighty world-power, created and administered by men, a great political engine under whose wheels the freedom and growth of the human spirit must be remorselessly crushed, a gigantic thing essentially of the earth earthy; or, on the other, the free recognition of an eternal First Principle, controlling, inspiring, disposing, condemning, approving the thoughts and actions of mankind, the spiritual communion of the human soul with the Invisible One, who is the absolute centre of Truth and Light and Love. Was not this truly a conflict between heaven and earth, between Christ and Antichrist? Could the Christian do otherwise than resist, even at the cost of his life, the blasphemous arrogance of a power which, in the Apostle's language, seated itself in the temple of God, showing itself that it is God? "To the Emperor," writes Tertullian, "we render such homage as is lawful for *us* and good for *him*, homage as to a man standing next to God, having received his all from God, and inferior to God alone." "I will not call him God, both because I cannot tell a lie myself, and because I dare not make him ridiculous." "I will not call him Lord except in the common acceptation of the word, and when I am not compelled to use it as synonymous with God; for I have but one Lord, God Almighty and Eternal, who is his God as well as mine."

"A free Church in a free State" has been the dream of more than one modern politician. It is only a dream, wholly incapable of realization. So far as the conception has any value, it must mean that Church and State shall work independently, both advancing *pari passu*, and neither interfering with the other. But the thing is impossible. The external bonds indeed may be severed for a time; but the State cannot liberate itself from the influence of the Church, and the Church cannot escape from the control of the State. Religious ideas, like scientific ideas, are in their very nature aggressive. Their aggressive attitude provokes resistance and invites repression. Where there is not an alliance there must be a collision. Indifference is impossible; and without indifference there can be no strict neutrality.

And so the gauntlet was thrown down, and the challenge accepted. For nearly two centuries and a half the struggle continued, till at length the persecutors retired baffled from the field. On the Christian side the combatants were twofold—those who fought with their pen and those who fought with their lives—the Apologists and the Martyrs. The history of Christianity in the second and third centuries is the history of these two bands of champions. The Apologists did their work well; but it was the Martyrs who achieved the victory.

And yet it must not be imagined that these persecutions were utterly relentless and persistent. The heathen magistrates, as a rule, were not disposed to extreme measures. When they persecuted, they did so because the political situation left them no choice. But, where magisterial prudence forbore, popular clamour stepped in. An extraordinary drought, or a pestilence, or an earthquake, or a famine, an inundation of the Tiber, or the failure of an inundation in the Nile, was attributed to the anger of the offended gods, and demanding the sacrifice of the Christians to appease them. In vain might the magistrates interpose to moderate the fury of the populace. The position of the Christians was illegal. The sword of the law hung quivering over them; and the slightest breath of excitement would snap the thread and bring it down on their bare necks.

It has been said lately, and said with some truth, that there is no practical mean between the policy of Alva and the policy of Gamaliel—between entire extirpation and absolute non-interference. All intermediate courses must be ineffectual; and, if ineffectual, they will only stimulate the opposition which they are intended to crush. The Roman government was not prepared to adopt either extreme in its treatment of the Christians. The policy of Gamaliel was absolutely excluded by their political necessities. The policy of Alva was either too troublesome to their natural indolence, or too repugnant to their humane instincts. At length, indeed, their fears were thoroughly aroused; the rapidly-growing numbers and influence of the sect alarmed them; and first under Decius, then under Diocletian, they resorted to extreme measures. But it was too late. The victory was already won.

And meanwhile these fitful, feverish, intermittent persecutions defeated their own ends. "Rack us, torture us, condemn us, mangle and crush us," writes Tertullian, "for your injustice is the attestation of our innocence. Therefore God suffers us to suffer these things. . . . And yet all your refinements of cruelty produce no effect. They rather stimulate the sect. We grow in numbers every time you mow us down. *Semen est sanguis Christianorum*—The blood of the Christians is seed sown. Many of your own philosophers exhort to the endurance of pain and death. Yet their words do not make as many disciples as the Christians by the teaching of their deeds. The very obstinacy with which you reproach us is your teacher. For who that contemplates it is not instigated to inquire what there is at the bottom of it? Who that inquires, does not embrace it? Who that embraces it, is not ready to suffer?"

But the numbers of the martyrs? Here we shall not find it easy to form any probable estimate. If it was the tendency of ancient hagiologers greatly to exaggerate these numbers, it is not less the tendency of modern critics unduly to underrate them. Nor is this a question of great moment. It may possibly be true that throughout the ten persecutions which ecclesiastical historians have recorded, the total number of martyrs was not so great as of those victims who were sacrificed to the ruthless policy of their Spanish masters during one single reign in the Netherlands in the sixteenth century, or of those soldiers who lost their lives on the battlefields of France in one single bloody campaign two years ago. Numbers are no adequate measure of the significance of any great event in history. The architectural effect of a building depends far more on the disposition of its parts and the fitness of its decorations, than on the hugeness of its masonry. I cannot consent to regard the battle of Marathon as a poor and insignificant atom in history, hardly worthy of attention, because the Greeks did not muster more than 10,000 men, and the number of their slain did not exceed 200. I feel bound to measure the importance of historical events by their moral significance and their moral results. And at Marathon I see the magnificent spectacle of a huge barbarian army under a barbarian tyrant repulsed and driven into the sea by a small band of courageous patriots, the champions of a free and progressive race; while the alternative which hung on the issue of those few hours' fighting with those scanty numbers in that circumscribed plain was not less critical than this, whether the freedom and civilization of Greece or the barbaric despotism of Persia was to shape the future destinies of the human race. And in the far more momentous conflict which we are now reviewing the standard must be the same. We measure its significance by the spirit of the combatants—their undaunted courage, their lofty self-devotion, their simple faith, their joyous hope.

It is enough that, whenever a sacrifice was demanded, a sacrifice was ready; that feeble girls and young children in the presence of death were nerved with the courage of heroes; that the Christian leaders not infrequently interposed to check the ardour which impelled men and women alike to rush headlong into martyrdom; that the heathen magistrates often desisted from sheer weariness when they saw the crowds pressing forward to suffer death for their religion. "Miserable wretches," said a Roman proconsul, baffled by their numbers, "if you want to die, you have precipices and ropes." It *did* seem strange that they would give their lives rather than conform, when conformity demanded so little—just to scatter a pinch of incense on the fire, or to swear by the genius of the emperor, or to say (they might unsay it the next moment if they wished) that they were not Christians. It was a new phenomenon—this strength made perfect in weakness. It arrested attention, and it compelled inquiry.

For no spectator could look on unmoved and indifferent at these scenes—whether it was the old man Ignatius, burning for the hour when he should confront the wild beasts in the Roman amphitheatre, entreating his friends not to intercede and rob him of the crown of martyrdom, trembling lest he should be found unworthy of this last seal of discipleship, uniting in himself the courage of a hero with the humility of a child; or the still more aged Polycarp, refusing to revile his Lord in that memorable saying, "Eighty-and-six years have I served Him, and He has done me no wrong; how then can I blaspheme my King and my Saviour?" and dying at the stake with the words of prayer and thanksgiving on his lips; or the boy Origen, thinking to lay down his life for his faith, his mother hiding his clothes that he might not expose himself to danger, and he himself writing to his father in prison to face death bravely and not to think of his family; or the slave girl Blandina, scourged, racked, and tortured day after day to extort a confession of guilt, thrown at length to the wild beasts, but protesting resolutely to the end, "I am Christian, and nothing wicked is done among us"; or that brave Christian wife who, when brought up to the altar by her pagan husband and forced to offer sacrifice, cried out indignantly, "*I* did not do it; *you* did it."

I wish that time would allow me to linger over these scenes, but I must draw to a close. Before concluding, however, I cannot forbear to direct your attention to a narrative, which is at once the most detailed, the most authentic, and the most touching of these early martyrologies. I only regret that the necessary abridgment will prevent me from doing justice to this simple and pathetic story.

The scene is Carthage or the neighbourhood; the probable year 202 A.D., during the reign of Severus; the occasion the Ides of March, the birthday of the Emperor's son the Cæsar Geta, when the amphitheatre demanded some human victims to grace the festival and to appease the populace. The victims are certain Christians, young men and young women. Among them Perpetua, a girlish matron of good birth, twenty-two years of age, with an infant child in her arms, and Felicitas, a female slave, herself also soon to become a mother. The martyrology consists partly of a diary written by the sufferers themselves while in prison, partly of an account drawn up by a Christian bystander, who witnessed the actual scene in the arena.

Perpetua was arrested. Her father, a heathen, entreated her to repudiate her faith. She pointed to an earthen vessel that stood by, and asked him, "Can you call this anything else but a pitcher?" "No." "Neither can I call myself by any other name than that which I am, a Christian." She was put into prison. "I was horrified," she writes in her diary, "for I had never experienced such darkness. O the cruel day! the oppressive heat from overcrowding! the insolent extortions of the soldiers! Above all I was racked with anxiety for my baby." But she soon recovered herself. "My prison," she says, "suddenly became like a palace, so that I would sooner have been there than anywhere else."

Then comes the record of a vision in answer to a prayer. She saw a golden ladder reaching to heaven. Its sides bristled with dangerous implements, knives, hooks, lances, which tore the flesh of any one who attempted to mount, if he were at all careless. At its foot was a huge dragon, lying in wait to scare away all who approached. She planted her foot on the monster's head, invoking the name of the Lord Jesus. She was helped up the ladder by a fellow-sufferer Saturus; and when she had mounted she was received and welcomed by one dressed like a shepherd, with white hair and of great stature. "So we knew," she adds, "that we must die, and we began to surrender all hope in this present world."

But her father continued to ply her with entreaties. He besought her to pity his gray hairs; to think of her brothers, of her mother, of her aunt, of her infant child who could not long survive her. He asked her to spare them all the disgrace of having a relation condemned as a criminal. He kissed her hand, threw himself at her feet, called her not his daughter, but his lady. She tried to comfort him, saying that she was in God's hands, not her own.

Then the day of trial came. The prisoners were placed in the dock. Again her father appeared, this time with her infant in his arms, entreating her to pity the child. The magistrate joined in his entreaties. He put the usual test questions, desiring to elicit an answer which might save her. But all in vain. "Offer sacrifice for the health of the Emperor." "I will *not* offer it." "Art thou a Christian?" "I am a Christian." She and her companions were condemned to the wild beasts, "And," she adds, "we went down to our prison glad of heart."

Then follows the record of visions, simply told, but instinct with beauty and meaning. They would perhaps be held superstitious by some. I dare not apply this term to them. They would well bear repeating, if time would allow.

At this point the interest of the narrative passes from Perpetua to her companion Felicitas. Felicitas is grieved lest her execution should be deferred on account of her condition. Her fellow-martyrs are very sad at the thought that they shall lose so dear a companion on their glorious journey. She and they pray that her delivery may be hastened. Their prayers are answered. A child is born in the prison. In the midst of her agony she cries out. "If you suffer so much pain now," says one of the attendants, "what will you do then when you are thrown to the wild beasts?" She answers, "Now I myself suffer what I suffer; but then there will be another in me who will suffer for me, because I shall suffer for Him."

The evening before the execution, according to

Roman custom, a supper was provided for the criminals with a cruel mockery of kindness, that they might forget their troubles in revelry. By these Christians this meal is converted, as far as circumstances permit, into an *agape*, or love-feast, the symbol and bond of Christian brotherhood. On such occasions the public were admitted that they might gratify a ghastly curiosity in scanning the looks and anatomizing the feelings of the miserable victims. Saturus, one of the martyrs, turned round fiercely upon these inquisitive bystanders. "Ay," said he, "note our features carefully, that you may know us again in that great day of Judgment." They were cowed by this rebuke; they retired; and many, we are told, believed.

The day came. Even the spectators shuddered when these two delicate women were led into the amphitheatre. Perpetua was the first victim. She was tossed by a furious heifer. Regaining her consciousness, she gathered her dress about her, and bound up her dishevelled hair, that she might not appear as one mourning in this her hour of glory. Then she gave a hand to her companion Felicitas, who had also been tossed, and raised her from the ground. Then, as if waking from sleep, she asked when they would be exposed to the furious creature. In her spiritual ecstasy she was unaware of what had happened. At length the signal was given by the spectators that they should receive the *coup de grace*. They rose up gladly, exchanged the last kiss of peace, and presented themselves to the executioner. The gladiator entrusted with this task was a novice; he wounded Perpetua slightly in the side by an ill-aimed blow; she directed the weapon in his hand towards her throat, and so she died.

Here I must close. Even this very imperfect treatment of an important subject will not have been without its use, if only for a few minutes this evening we have realized the presence of the noble army of martyrs, the great cloud of witnesses who throng round the arena of our conflicts, the silent but sympathetic spectators of our trials and our victories.

III

On the two preceding Tuesdays I discussed the relations of the early Christian to the world without, first as a member of society, and secondly as a unit in the State. In this third and concluding lecture I shall consider his relations to the Church. We have watched him hitherto in the heat of the conflict with external powers; we shall see him now arming himself for the struggle in the privacy of the Christian brotherhood. My subject this evening will be Christian life within the Christian body, and more especially Christian worship as the soul of that life.

To the careless heathen bystander this inner life of the Christian was strangely anomalous and perplexing. Such glimpses as he might accidentally obtain revealed a state of things of which he had no experience, and to which he could attach no meaning. He found nothing on which the eye or the hand could fasten. It was all so vague, so unsubstantial, so intangible and elusive. There were no external emblems and no imposing rites, without which religion seemed to him to be an impossibility.

Again and again the heathen antagonists of Christianity give expression to their surprise in the same taunting language, "You have no images, no altars, no temples." The principal squares and streets of Rome or Athens were lined with sanctuaries and dotted with altars; public thoroughfares and private houses were thronged with statues of gods and demigods; the language of the common people bristled with invocations of deities; the air reeked from time to time with the fat of victims or the fumes of incense. When Caligula ascended the imperial throne the festivities extended over three whole months, and 160,000 victims were sacrificed in Rome alone. When during the reign of M. Aurelius a deadly pestilence broke out, the Emperor summoned to the metropolis the priests of all religions, national and foreign, and the city was given over to lustrations, sacrifices, and rites of every kind and every country. To all this the bald simplicity of Christian worship stood in marked contrast.

Even the Jews presented a religious problem which the heathen found it difficult to solve. He was perplexed to learn that they had no external object of worship. But at all events they had a temple rich with marble and gold; they had altars smoking with sacrifices; they had priests arrayed in priestly robes. Here was something which he could understand. But in Christianity he found nothing of the kind. A silent mysterious gathering at stated times in some obscure private dwelling seemed to exhaust the religion of this anomalous sect.

His inference, though strangely at fault, was not altogether unnatural. These Christians, he supposed, were *Atheists*. Under cover of religion they were hatching some vile conspiracy. He had stumbled on another of those secret clubs, those illegal associations, which his jealous suspicions were ever on the watch to detect.

This strange misconception he persistently maintained. Atheism was the indictment brought against Flavius Clemens, the cousin of Domitian, when he was condemned to death for his adhesion to the new faith. "Away with the Atheists!" was the common war-cry of the persecutor. In vain the Apologists attempted to explain. "What image can I make of God," wrote one, "when rightly considered man himself is God's image? What temple can I build to Him, when the whole world wrought by His handiwork cannot contain Him? . . . The offering acceptable to Him is an honest spirit and a pure mind and a sincere conscience. These are our sacrifices; these are God's rites. Thus with us he is the better worshipper who is the more upright man. By this we believe that God is, because we can apprehend Him, though we cannot see Him." To all such explanations the heathen had a ready answer, "Show us your God." This seemed to put an end to the controversy. The Christian could not satisfy the test. He had nothing to show; nothing which in the eyes of the heathen counted for religion; nothing but a firm faith and a heroic courage and clean hands and a blameless life.

From these notices it is evident that during the early centuries the ritual of the Christians was very simple. One point at least seems clear, that they were not yet in the habit of erecting buildings devoted solely to divine worship.

This, however, was not a principle of their faith, but rather a necessity of their position. As a corporation they were not recognized by the law; it was therefore impossible for them to hold corporate property. Moreover, common prudence would deter them from any display which might arouse the fury of the populace, or invite the repression of the magistrates. Hence there is not, so far as I am aware, any explicit notice of a church erected either at Rome or in the provinces before the close of the second century. Beyond the limits of the Empire the case would be different. In Syria, for instance, where the kings of Edessa early embraced Christianity, no such restraints would be imposed upon the Christians. Accordingly, as early as the year 202, when a sudden inundation swept over the city of Edessa, destroying the royal palace, the city walls, and other important buildings, the "temple of the Church of the Christians" is mentioned among the edifices thus demolished. The expression points to a building of some pretensions. How long it had been standing we do not know; but there is no reason to suppose that it was either the first or the only erection of the kind. But meanwhile, in the Metropolis and in the great cities of the Empire, the meetings for public worship would be held in a commodious room attached to the residence of some private Christian. "Where do you assemble?" asks the Roman prefect of Justin Martyr, when brought before him for trial. "Where each man will and can; thinkest thou that we all meet in the same place?" is the reply. "Tell me," the prefect urges again, "where do you assemble; in what place dost thou gather thy disciples together?" "I have lodged," he replies, "over the house of Martin at the Timotine bath during the whole of my present stay. This is my second visit to the city of Rome; and I know no other place of meeting besides his house." A period of a century and a quarter has now elapsed since those first gatherings of the Apostles after the Resurrection; yet still the disciples, as of old, meet in an upper room, for fear, not now of the Jews, but of the Gentiles.

But when the first quarter of the third century had run out, their condition was much improved. The favour which Alexander Severus showed towards them could not fail to produce an immediate effect. The answer of this emperor, when a dispute arose between the Christians and the licensed victuallers about the possession of a certain piece of ground in Rome, is well known. "It is better," he said, "that God should be worshipped in the place in whatever manner, than that it should be given over to the victuallers." Such a verdict from such lips would naturally give a great impulse to church-building. Yet notwithstanding, so long as they were unrecognized by the law, their tenure was altogether precarious. The disability, however, was soon removed. About the year 260 the Emperor Gallienus issued a rescript prohibiting any interference with the Christians, and expressly restoring to them their "places of worship." By this rescript all obstacles to the multiplication of churches were at length removed.

Thus we find ourselves confronted by a broad fact, which cannot fail to suggest important reflections. During the first century and a half of its existence, Christianity in the Roman Empire had no churches, as we understand the term; while throughout the next half-century such buildings were rare and unobtrusive. Yet all this while its numbers were rapidly increasing, till it had invaded every part of the Empire, and counted its converts in every rank and department of life.

Living in an age when every church and every sect sets apart for divine worship buildings erected with some pretensions to architectural effect, when every considerable town in every Christian country bristles with the towers and spires of edifices consecrated to prayer—assembled, as we are this evening, under this glorious dome in a Cathedral which justly reckons among the masterpieces of creative genius—

we cannot fail to be struck with the contrast between the present and the past. Can it be, we are led to ask, that these later forms of worship are a perversion of the simplicity of the Gospel ? that we have entirely departed from the principles of primitive Christianity in the elaborate development of our architecture, our music, our ritual ? A moment's reflection will check this hasty inference which we might be tempted to draw from the contrast. I have already said that this feature in early Christianity was not a deliberate choice, but an enforced abstention. I would now urge (for this consideration is still more important) that it was also a necessary discipline, a providential design, in the early education of the Church. An example will serve to illustrate my meaning. To ourselves the stern prohibition, which some early Christian teachers placed upon the study of the ancient authors, may appear at once superfluous and illiberal. We can read our Homer or our Virgil without the slightest danger of being seduced into the worship of Zeus or Apollo ; but when heathen mythology was still a living power, exercising a fatal fascination over the minds of men, the license, which we rightly claim for ourselves, might have been disastrous in the extreme. And similarly in the case before us. I pointed out in an earlier lecture how polytheism insinuated itself into every department of public duty and every corner of domestic life. But while thus ubiquitous and intrusive, it was essentially external. It made large demands on its worshippers; but these demands were confined to conformity in outward rites. It did not appeal to the heart, and it did not reform the life. The heathen did not understand religion as a moral and spiritual influence. His only conception of it was as an elaborate system of sacrifices, lustrations, auspices; a multiplication of shrines and a multiplication of deities. It was necessary, for the future of the Church, that the Christian should break once for all with the spirit of paganism. By the stern teaching of an imperious necessity, he was weaned from this false and low conception of religion. The external symbols and appliances—the buildings, the music, the paintings, and the sculptures—which may be innocent and useful to us, were denied, or almost denied, to him, that, thus thrown back upon his own spiritual resources, he might lay the foundations of a spiritual fabric. This training was to the infancy of the Church what the careful seclusion and the enforced simplicity of life is to the infancy of the individual— the necessary discipline of the child for the freedom and the development of manhood. Much that would have been injurious then, is useful—we might almost say, is indispensable—now. But ever and again in the history of the Church there have been epochs when ritual has run to excess, when the spiritual life of the Church has been threatened with suffocation from the pressure of external forms. Then a terrible reaction ensues. The iconoclast and the puritan break into the sanctuary, sweeping away in their indiscriminate zeal much that is beautiful and edifying and useful, leaving desolation in their train. Good and devout men mourn over the wholesale work of destruction; but it is God's own chastisement, who will not allow His limits to be overstepped, and vindicates the spirituality of His Gospel at the cost of much individual pain and no little immediate loss.

Of the simple ritual which sufficed before the age of church-building began, a valuable notice is preserved in the Apologist Justin.

"On the day called Sunday," he writes, "all those who live in the towns or in the country meet together; and the memoirs of the Apostles and the writings of the Prophets are read, as long as time allows. Then, when the reader has ended, the president addresses words of instruction and exhortation to imitate these good things. Then we all stand up together and offer prayers. And when prayer is ended, bread is brought and wine and water, and the president offers up alike prayers and thanksgivings with all his energy (or ability), and the people give their assent saying the Amen; and the distribution of the elements, over which the thanksgiving has been pronounced, is made so that each partakes; and to those who are absent they are sent by the hands of the deacons. And those who have the means and are so disposed give as much as they will, each according to his inclination; and the sum collected is placed in the hands of the president, who himself succours the orphans and widows, and those who through sickness or any other cause are in want, and the prisoners, and the foreigners who are staying in the place, and, in short, he provides for all who are in need." Justin then goes on to explain why Sunday is selected for these assemblies, as the day at once of the Creation from chaos and of the Resurrection of Christ from the dead. And he adds in conclusion: "If these proceedings seem to you agreeable to reason and truth, pay respect to them; but if they seem to be foolishness, then treat them with contempt as foolish things, and do not condemn to death as enemies those who are guilty of no crime."

This notice requires little or no comment. You will have observed that Justin's description of primitive worship, written more than seventeen centuries ago, contains all those elements which to the present time are held requisite to the completeness of divine service: the reading of the Gospels and the Prophets, lessons from the Old and the New Testament; the words of exhortation, or sermon; the prayers and thanksgivings, the minister leading and the congregation responding; and lastly, as the climax to which all the previous service leads up, the Eucharistic celebration, the Holy Communion, which is the supreme act of Christian worship, at once the strongest pledge of brotherly love and the highest means of spiritual grace.

In some points we may trace divergences from

the present usage of our own or other churches. Thus, for instance, the attitude of prayer is a standing position, following the common practice in ancient times. Thus, again, it is difficult to say how far the prayers and thanksgivings were written or extempore, but it seems that the latter was not altogether excluded. And again, the Eucharistic wine was diluted with water. It was commonly taken so in ancient banquets; and in the Christian festival a symbolic reference to the water and the blood would recommend the mixing for this sacred purpose. But these are minor details, not affecting the main character of the service. In all essentials we are struck with the *continuity* of Christian worship, when we compare its primitive form in this earliest record with its latest developments as we witness them ourselves.

But I cannot dismiss this subject without calling your attention to the practical measures which flowed immediately from these gatherings for worship. The collection of alms to be distributed to the orphan and the prisoner, to the sick and the stranger, is regarded by Justin as an inseparable part of divine service. His narrative seems to put in a working shape the Apostle's maxim, "He that loveth not his brother whom he hath seen, how can he love God whom he hath not seen?" Without practical benevolence there can be no true worship. "He prayeth best who loveth best."

How fully alive the early Christians were to this

truth of truths, this notice at once suggests. It exemplifies that distinguishing feature of Christianity which we may call its chivalry. By chivalry I mean the temper which throws its shield over the weak, which looks upon inability as its special charge, which finds its highest satisfaction in helping those who cannot help themselves. If we cast an eye over any Christian country now, we find it dotted over with ragged schools, orphanages, reformatories, hospitals, convalescent homes, idiot asylums, charitable institutions of all kinds for the relief of misery and helplessness and want. Such appliances seem to us the indispensable accompaniments of an advanced stage of society; for without these compensations, imperfect as they are, the inequalities of social life, aggravated by a high state of civilization, would become intolerable. Yet when we look back to the great days of ancient Rome, befôre the example of the Christians had begun to tell upon the heathen, we can hardly see the faintest traces of any such institutions.

Their foundations were laid in those quiet little prayer meetings held every seventh day in a retired upper chamber of some humble quarter like the Trastevere, in the careless, magnificent, pleasure-seeking city.

But before the age of church-building began, Christian worship had been localized in an unexpected quarter, dictated partly by a sentiment of piety and partly by the force of circumstances.

The scene now changes from the vacant room in a private dwelling to the dark passages and chambers of an underground cemetery.

While the Roman law strictly prohibited the erection of churches by the Christians, it offered no impediment to the foundation of cemeteries. The honours paid to the dead were a main element in the religion of the Roman. He scrupulously respected the rights of sepulture in the case of others, as he valued them in his own.

A Roman of the middle classes would, almost as a matter of course, belong to some burial-club or guild or confraternity, which provided for the due performance of the last offices over him on his decease. These guilds were recognized and enrolled by the government. The bond of union was various; the members would belong to the same family or the same locality or the same trade. Sometimes the link of connexion would be purely sentimental, or even altogether arbitrary. Each guild had its own burial-place, which was duly surveyed and registered by the State.

The Christians would have no more difficulty than any other body in forming such associations. The Romans, indeed, were accustomed to burn their dead at this time; while Christian sentiment dictated burial as the right mode of sepulture, reproducing, as it does, the Apostolic image of the seed sown in the ground, to spring up hereafter into a new and luxuriant life. But this fact presented no obstacle to their recognition, and indeed would hardly provoke a remark. The Jews also buried their dead, and yet they were freely recognized. Indeed, this had till very lately been the common practice with the Romans themselves. The ancient usage still lingered in some places. It was still recognized by an old law—perhaps disused, though not repealed—which directed that, when a body was burned, one limb should be cut off and buried in the earth.

Of this privilege, which the Roman law of sepulture extended to them, the Christians gladly availed themselves. If they were refused recognition collectively as Christians, they might obtain it sectionally as burial-clubs. Their religion was prohibited, but their sepulture was free. The first occasion on which a Roman bishop appears in any official relation to the government is in the earliest years of the third century, when Callistus, then Archdeacon of Rome, as president of one of these guilds, takes charge of the catacomb which still bears his name. This was not the earliest, but it is the most famous of the catacombs.

But what is a catacomb? Before answering this question, I will ask you to accompany me on a visit to the great Appian Way which spans the Campagna southward from Rome. The Romans were the great road-makers of the world, and the Appian is confessedly the queen of roads. You will remember Milton's description of the pageantry which thronged this great thoroughfare of nations—

> "The conflux issuing forth, or entering in :
> Prætors, proconsuls to their provinces
> Hasting, or on return, in robes of state ;
> Lictors and rods, the ensigns of their power ;
> Legions and cohorts, turms of horse and wings ;
> Or embassies from regions far remote,
> In various habits."

Far away this road stretches in one long straight unbroken line, across the plain, up the hill slope which bars the horizon, till dipping below the summit it is lost to the eye. On either side, for a distance of ten or twelve miles at least, it is lined with splendid monuments of various designs—some so huge that they served as fortresses in the middle ages, others smaller in size, but all alike, or almost all, betokening lavish expenditure or artistic skill. I am speaking of the time with which we are immediately concerned—the second and third centuries of the Christian era; but even now, if you visit this famous Way, as I have visited it, on some fine bright winter afternoon, when the sun is low in the west, and these dismantled wrecks of the past, rising up gaunt and spectre-like, fling across the ancient pavement their long shadows jagged by the ancient kerbstones, which still fence it in—even now, in its forlorn and rueful state, faded and stripped, it impresses the imagination with a sense of past magnificence and beauty, which I dare not hope by any description of mine to reproduce. And these are the sepulchres of the mighty dead of Rome—the Scipios, the Servilii, the Metelli, men who won for themselves an undying name in the records of their country.

I will now ask you to visit a very different scene. You are still on this same road, and about a mile and a half from the city gate you diverge. Then, passing through a narrow doorway and down a steep flight of steps, you find yourself in a catacomb. The contrast is as great as could well be imagined. You have suddenly exchanged the light and splendour of a great Roman thoroughfare, its architectural beauty and its lavish magnificence, for an interminable warren of dark subterranean vaults and passages. This is the Christian place of sepulture, as the other was the heathen. You examine it more narrowly. You find that it is an endless labyrinth of long narrow galleries, intersecting each other nearly at right angles, and extending you know not how far. Here and there (but these are rare exceptions) they open out into small chambers. As you grope your way by the uncertain aid of a torch or a candle (for there is no light from the upper air), you see that these passages are lined on both sides from the floor to the roof with long, low, horizontal niches excavated in the native rock, rising one above another in tiers, like the shelves in a wardrobe or the berths in a ship's cabin. There will generally be five or six of these tiers, sometimes as many as twelve. Each contains a dead body. They are hermetically sealed, and the slab which covers them is inscribed with a name. But this investigation has not exhausted the extent of the catacomb. As yet you are only traversing its first floor; there is yet another story arranged in the same way, to which you descend by another flight of steps; and again another and another. In the catacomb of St. Callistus, which apparently dives deepest into the bowels of the earth, not less than six successive floors are found. Now read the inscriptions: you will find them ill-composed, ill-written, not infrequently ill-spelt, half Latin, half Greek. Or look at the paintings (for there are paintings here and there in the chambers): they are very rude for the most part, inartistic in design and clumsy in execution, showing neither a cultivated imagination nor a practised hand.

I have introduced you to one catacomb, which will serve as a type of all. If you extend your search you will find that these subterranean cemeteries encircle Rome with a vast girdle, which, roughly speaking, passes between the second and third milestone from the gates, intersecting the great roads which radiate from the city like spokes of a wheel, and from which access is gained to these several lodging-houses of the dead. In this zone the ground is honeycombed with their labyrinthine corridors and chambers, hollowed out in the soft tufa stone, the deposit of extinct volcanoes in prehistoric ages. Wherever this tufa is neither too hard to be easily and inexpensively worked, nor too soft to sustain when excavated the superincumbent weight, a catacomb is almost sure to be found. It has been estimated that the united length of all these galleries would amount to three hundred and fifty, to six hundred, even to eight hundred or nine hundred miles. All such estimates must be regarded only as very rough conjectures, as their wide difference shows; but they will enable us in some degree to realize the enormous number of bodies which are congregated in this vast city of the dead.

We have visited in succession the necropolis of the heathen and the cemetery of the Christian, the Appian Way above ground, and the Appian Way beneath the soil; and we have marked the startling contrast. This contrast, one might say, is in all respects unfavourable to the Christians. On the one hand you have the free air, the bright sunshine, the blue sky, the lavish expenditure of wealth, the display of constructive and decorative skill—in short, all the advantages of nature and all the appliances of art combined. All here is intelligence and beauty and brightness and magnificence. Can we add, all is cheerfulness? On the other hand, when you dive into the Christian cemetery, you have none of these things; all the accompaniments of the place are utterly depressing, you would say: illiterate inscriptions, rude paintings, a damp close atmosphere, an impenetrable prison-like gloom. All is monotony, confinement, darkness—and you might be tempted to add, all is despair. But your curiosity is aroused, and you study and compare the sepulchral inscriptions of these two cities of the dead. The epitaphs of a people or an age are no treacherous indications of its mind. And here a study of these voices from the past entirely reverses your first crude impression. With all its light and splendour, the utterance of the above-ground necropolis is one long wail of despair: there are touching expressions of natural affection, beautiful in themselves, but not one ray of glory pierces the dark cold shadow of death. Hopelessness, utter hopelessness, is traced in every line. The external magnificence is like the jewels and the finery which render more ghastly by contrast the bloodless features of the corpse which they bedeck. Turn to the Christian inscriptions, and all is changed. Neither bad grammar nor defective orthography, nor rude art nor cramped space, nor damp nor darkness can dim or distort the light with which the consciousness of an immortality floods and glorifies these subterranean vaults. All here is joy and brightness and hope. The often-repeated inscription "In peace" tells its own tale. The paintings are all conceived in the same spirit. Now it is the dove or the palm branch, emblems of love, of innocence, and of victory. Now it is the Good Shepherd, tenderly bearing on his shoulders the feeble or the maimed one of the flock. And now again it is a heathen subject adopted and transfigured by a Christian baptism. Orpheus, thrilling, entrancing, dissolving the souls of men with the ecstasies of his unearthly music—not failing now to "quite set free His half-regained" spouse, but presenting her, ransomed and sanctified without spot or wrinkle before the Eternal throne, triumphing over death on His cross and in His grave, and thus in a new and a higher sense

"Making Hell grant what Love did seek."

And even when subjects of a more painful interest are chosen, and the Christian is reminded of the persecutions which he may be called at any moment to endure, they are still treated in a manner which suggests the anticipation of victory. The favourite themes are Daniel praying fearlessly among the hungry lions, and the Three Children singing the song of praise in the flames of the heated furnace. The catacombs signally vindicate the Apostolic law of "strength made perfect in weakness."

It has often been assumed that these underground cemeteries were the common places of assembly for the Christians. This seems to be a mistake. The space is too confined and the arrangement too inconvenient for any large gathering of people. Nor indeed was it necessary in ordinary times to resort to such obscure hiding-places. If he were only careful not to provoke interference, the Christian might generally hold his meetings unmolested in the upper air. But in seasons of trouble and danger the catacomb was at once the asylum of the fugitive and the church of the worshipper. A Roman's respect for the dead would generally secure these cemeteries from molestation. But when the fury of the populace was aroused, even these sanctuaries were invaded. It was a new aggravation of wrong when, in the Valerian persecution, these cemeteries were invaded by authority, and the Christians hunted down in their hiding-places. But cruelties which the government was slow to adopt were often anticipated by the violence of the people. An inscription from a catacomb, purporting to belong to the reign of Antoninus, gives a lively picture of these moments of terror. "Alexander," so it runs, "is not dead, but lives beyond the stars, though his body rests in this tomb. Bending his knees to offer sacrifice to the true God, he is led away to execution. O unhappy times, when amidst worship and prayer we cannot be safe even in caves. What is more wretched than life; yet what is more wretched in death than to be denied burial by friends and parents?" At such times the fugitives would secure their hiding-places by walling off corridors and blocking up entrances, while they provided an egress by piercing some new passage into the upper air.

But the Christian was drawn to the catacombs not less by the sentiment of piety than by the instinct of self-preservation. For here were the graves of the martyrs. It is painful to think how very soon the reverence for the heroism and saintliness of those who had suffered for the faith degenerated into a mere worship of relics. But I speak now of a time when a healthier tone prevailed. The memory of their sufferings was yet too fresh, and the sympathy of the living with the dead too real, for any very gross corruption of a sentiment so pure and noble. As the survivors met in some underground chamber over the grave of a martyred friend, and consecrated the eucharistic elements on the very slab which covered his remains, carrying their own lives in their hands, and eating their Christian passover, as of old, in haste and trembling, their loins girt and their feet shod, expecting at any moment the alarm which should summon them forth on their last long. journey, they could not but feel themselves one with those who had gone before, one in their sympathies, one in their struggles, one in their hopes. The barrier between death and life dissolves before a great crisis which reveals the Eternal Presence. At such moments the continuity of existence is felt. The Christian realizes his communion with the past and the future; and feeling that he is no more an isolated unit floating in a boundless void, he nerves himself with that strength of purpose and that assurance of hope which the sense of association alone can give.

With this thought, which though old is ever new, I will conclude. If I have succeeded in exciting in any one member of this congregation a desire for a more familiar acquaintance with the records of his spiritual ancestry in primitive times; if I have struck out in one intelligent heart a fresh spark of sympathy with the grand historic past; if only a single hearer has carried away from these lectures, into the fretting cares and distractions and trials of daily life, one cheering memory or one heroic resolve or one ennobling thought, then the task which I set to myself has been more than accomplished. I could have desired nothing more.

COMPARATIVE PROGRESS OF ANCIENT AND MODERN MISSIONS

It is hardly possible to glance over the columns of a newspaper, or to overhear a conversation in society, where the subject is discussed, without encountering some expression of impatience at the slow progress of modern missions; and not infrequently it will be stated that they are an acknowledged failure.

Now it is my conviction that this disappointment is quite as unreasonable as it is faithless. I believe that all such misgivings will melt before a thorough investigation of facts; that if we would lay this spectre of ill success, we need only the courage to face it; and, above all, that an appeal to history will dispel any gloomy forebodings on this score. It will be found, if I mistake not, that the resemblances of early and recent missions are far greater than their contrasts; that both alike have had to surmount the same difficulties and been chequered by the same vicissitudes; that both alike exhibit the same inequalities of progress, the same alternations of success and failure, periods of acceleration followed by periods of retardation, when the surging wave has been sucked back in the retiring current, while yet the flood has been rising steadily all along, though the unobservant eye might fail to mark it, advancing towards that final consummation when the earth shall be covered with the knowledge of the Lord as the waters cover the sea. History is an excellent cordial for the drooping courage.

To history, therefore, I make my appeal. And yet here I am impressed with the difficulties which beset my path. Any one who has endeavoured to arrive at definite results respecting the progress of Christianity in the early and middle ages must be struck with the paucity of data. It is only here and there that he finds a statistical fact on which, as on firm standing ground, he can plant his foot securely. For the rest, hypothetical combinations and plausible analogies must be summoned to fill up the void. Yet out of all this uncertainty, unless I am deceived, enough of fact will emerge to justify an inference and to point a moral.

As a starting-point to my comparison of the present and the past, I shall try to ascertain the proportion of the Christian population to the whole human race at two different epochs. The one point of time shall be the middle of the third century, when the Gospel had been preached for nearly two centuries and a quarter, amid all the discouragements of a worldly opposition, but with all the zeal of a new-born enthusiasm ; the other, the age in which we live, when it has passed through a chequered career of almost eighteen centuries and a half.

Now I have compared the estimates given by several able statisticians of the proportion which the Christians bear to the whole human race at the present time or in the present generation, and I find that it is generally reckoned at a little more or at a little less than one-third of the whole. This is pretty nearly the estimate of Wiggers and of Berghaus.[1] One authority, however, places it at one-fifth.[2] To avoid exaggeration, I will take the lowest estimate.

For the statistics of the earlier epoch which I propose to take, I am mainly indebted to Gibbon's investigations. These I have examined step by step; and though it is impossible to feel anything like absolute certainty about the result, yet I have not found reason to question the general truth of his calculations. At all events, nothing has yet been alleged on the opposite side which deserves the same attention. What, then, are the facts?

Setting aside the rhetorical passages of Tertullian

---

[1] Wiggers (1842) reckons the Christians at 228 millions out of 657 millions; Berghaus (1852) at 30·7 per cent. It is plain that so long as statisticians differ in their estimates of the whole population of the globe by several hundred millions, all attempts at establishing a proportion must be most precarious. The element of uncertainty, however, is not in the Christian so much as in the non-Christian portion.

[2] Sondermann, in the *Church Missionary Society's Atlas*, where other estimates also will be found.

and other writers,[1] which I will not venture with Gibbon to characterize as "splendid exaggerations," but which, even if taken literally, bear witness, with one exception, rather to the wide diffusion than to the overflowing numbers of the Christians, we turn to statements at once more sober and more definite.

Origen wrote his treatise against Celsus about the year 246, when the Church had enjoyed a long period of uninterrupted peace, so that circumstances had been peculiarly favourable to her growth. Speaking of the efficacy of the prayers of the Christians, he asks what might not be expected "if not only a very few indeed (πάνυ ὀλίγοι) were to agree, as now, but all the subjects of the Roman Empire."[2] To a Christian the proportion of the Christians would appear larger than it actually was; for they would occupy the foreground in his field of view. It is no insignificant fact, therefore, that Origen should speak of them as a very small fraction of the Empire.[3]

[1] Justin, *Dial.* c. 117; Tertull. *Apol.* 37; *Adv. Jud.* 7; see Gibbon, ii. p. 369 seq. I believe that if any one will read these passages carefully, making the same allowance for the rhetoric of enthusiasm which he would make in a parliamentary speech or a missionary sermon, he will see that they are not inconsistent with the conclusions at which I have arrived below.

[2] *c. Cels.* viii. 69 (i. p. 794, Delarue).

[3] On the other hand, Blunt, *First Three Centuries*, p. 209 seq., quotes other passages from Origen, in which, like Justin and Tertullian, he speaks of the wide diffusion and great numbers of the Christians. These passages must be taken for what they are worth; but they cannot seriously invalidate the testimony of an incidental notice such as I have quoted. Origen's words (*c. Cels.* i. 27), it is right to add, are not nearly so strong in the original as they appear in Mr. Robertson's quotation (i. p. 152).

Though Origen's statement is general, he more especially represents the flourishing Church of Alexandria. Not very different is the impression derived from a notice relating to Asia Minor. Gregory Thaumaturgus, a pupil of Origen, was appointed to the see of Neocæsarea, the most important town, if not the metropolis, of Pontus, about the year 240. After working on for about a quarter of a century with marvellous success, he was able to express his thankfulness at the close of his life that he only left seventeen heathens in the town and neighbourhood, though when he went there he had found only as many Christians.[1] We are not perhaps required to take his statement literally, but after all reasonable deductions it is plain that the Christians then formed only a minute and inappreciable fraction of the population in one of the largest towns in Asia Minor—so minute, perhaps, that they would pass unnoticed in the mass of their heathen fellow-citizens.[2]

---

[1] Greg. Nyss. *Op.* iii. p. 574 seq. ; comp. Basil *de Spir. Sanct.* iii. p. 63. The passages are referred to in Tillemont, iv. p. 327. The saying of Gregory Thaumaturgus is reported, as I have given it in the text, by Gregory Nyssen. On the other hand, Basil inverts his brother's mode of statement, and says expressly that there were only seventeen Christians in Neocæsarea when Gregory Thaumaturgus entered upon his charge. I have felt bound to prefer the account of the former, as being less favourable to my own views and as inherently more probable.

[2] Gibbon glances at, but does not solve, the difficulty of reconciling this notice with the account which Pliny gives, more than a century and a quarter earlier, of the rapid spread of Christianity in these parts. The explanation seems to be twofold : (1) It is clear from his own account that the judicious persecution which

From Asia Minor I turn to Rome. In the capital, there is every reason to think, the Christians were as influential, and bore as large a proportion to the heathen population, as in any part of the Empire, except possibly some districts of Africa, and some exceptional cities elsewhere, such as Antioch. Now in an extant letter of Cornelius,[1] who was Bishop of Rome from 250 to 252, it is stated that the number of widows and others receiving the alms of the Church was over 1500. Unfortunately the whole number of the Christians is not recorded; but in the Church of Antioch, somewhat later, we find that the proportion of these recipients of alms was three for every hundred.[2] Assuming this same proportion to hold for Rome[3] (and there is at all events no reason

Pliny himself instituted was very effective, and perhaps later persecutions also may have done their work. (2) There was a strong pagan revival in the middle of the second century, which, backed by the zeal and personal character of the Antonines, made great progress in several parts. On this latter point see Friedländer, *Sittengeschichte Roms*, iii. p. 430.

[1] Euseb. *H. E.* vi. 43. Cornelius also states that there were in the Roman Church 46 presbyters, 7 deacons, 7 sub-deacons, 42 acolytes, and 50 readers, exorcists, and porters.

[2] St. Chrysostom (vii. p. 810, ed. Bened.) reckons the number of the Christians at Antioch, on a rough calculation (οἶμαι), at 100,000. In another passage (vii. p. 658) he states that the number of widows and virgins receiving the alms of the Church there is 3000. As the progress of Christianity was less rapid among the wealthier classes in the earlier ages than in the later, we are almost certainly on the safe side when we apply to the middle of the third century this proportion which belongs to the end of the fourth. It should be added, that Cornelius includes others besides widows and virgins in the 1500.

[3] Gibbon remarks in his note (ii. p. 366) that this proportion was first fixed for Rome by Burnet, and approved by Moyle, though they were ignorant of the passage in Chrysostom. He adds that this passage "converts their conjecture almost into a fact."

for supposing it less), we should get 50,000 as the whole number of Roman Christians. Now, at the very lowest estimate the population of Rome amounted to one million (some make it a million and a half),[1] so that the Christians at this time would form somewhat less than one-twentieth of the whole. This is Gibbon's estimate, and, so far as I am able to judge, it errs on the side of excess rather than of defect. At all events the sepulchral monuments do not suggest anything like this proportion. The extant Christian inscriptions, which can certainly be referred to the second and third centuries, may almost be counted on the fingers, while the heathen inscriptions of the same period must reckon by hundreds or thousands. In De Rossi's collection of early Christian inscriptions in Rome, I find that only nine are included prior to the middle of the third century. Of these, several are assumed to be Christian from certain indications without definite proof, and the earliest, which is quite indisputable, belongs to the year 234.[2]

From Rome again I pass to Gaul. It is recorded in the martyrology of Saturninus, who was appointed Missionary Bishop of Toulouse in the year 250, that at this time " only a church had been raised here

[1] For estimates of the population of Rome see Friedländer, *Sittengeschichte Roms*, i. p. 23 ; Becker and Marquardt, *Röm. Alterth.* iii. 2, p. 101.
[2] On the other hand, some of those included among the collections of heathen inscriptions may have been Christian, though they give no indication of the fact.

ANCIENT AND MODERN MISSIONS 79

and there in some cities " of Gaul "by the devotion of a few Christians."[1] It is true that more than two generations before the martyrdoms at Vienne and Lyons bear witness to the presence of many zealous Christians in those cities; but these, as may be gathered from the narrative, were chiefly Greek and Asiatic settlers.[2] In the middle of the third century, then, we may reasonably infer that native Gaul was not more Christian than native India is at the present time.

These facts relate to some of the principal cities of the Empire; and if the proportion of the Christians even in these was so small, what must it have been in the rural districts? The word "pagan" tells its own tale. Long after the inhabitants of the cities had been converted to Christianity, the peasant still remained a synonym for the unbeliever.

From such notices as these Gibbon argues that at the time of Constantine's conversion not more than a twentieth part of the subjects of the Empire had enlisted themselves under the banner of the

[1] Ruinart, *Act. Sinc. Mart.* p. 130. "Raræ in aliquibus civitatibus ecclesiæ paucorum Christianorum devotione consurgerent."

[2] Euseb. v. i. The date of the letter in which these martyrdoms are recorded is 177 A.D. The points to be observed are: (1) that the names of the sufferers are Greek or Latin; (2) that two are distinctly stated to have come from Asia Minor; (3) that the letter is addressed to the "brethren of Asia and Phrygia," evidently because these latter were nearly interested in the incidents; (4) that the Churches of Gaul at this time are known to have been indebted to Asia Minor for their leaders, as *e.g.* in the case of Irenæus.

Cross, and this on "the most favourable calculation."[1] Of the age of Constantine I dare affirm nothing, for the notices do not refer to this late date; and, moreover, there are indications of a rapid increase during the interval; but at the time of which I am speaking, the middle of the third century, we may feel tolerably confident that we are overstating the proportion if we reckon the Christians at one-twentieth of the subjects of the Empire.[2]

And if so, what was this proportion to the population of the whole world? Here we have to take account of the densely-peopled empires of the East, such as India and China; we have to reckon in the swarming tribes of barbarians who poured down upon the Empire in countless hordes from the north and north-east, within a very few years; we have to allow for the unexplored regions of Africa, the unknown western hemisphere, the countless islands of the ocean. Should we then be wronging the Empire if we estimated its subjects as constituting

[1] ii. p. 372. Schaff, *History of the Christian Church*, i. p. 152, estimates the proportion at one-tenth; Robertson (i. p. 156), whose estimate seems to be as high as any, at one-fifth. I abstain from conjecture where there is an absence of data; but attention should be directed to the fact that the spread of Christianity appears to have been very rapid between the Decian and Diocletian persecutions, in the last half of the third century.

[2] Even if the proportion were three or four fold greater, which is highly improbable, it would be difficult to justify the language held by the leading journal in an article on the day of Intercession: "Once on a time a man (*i.e.* St. Paul) landed on the shores of Europe determined to convert it, and he did convert, for his work is done after some sort, if not quite as it should be."

ANCIENT AND MODERN MISSIONS 81

from one-seventh to one-tenth of the whole population of the globe? If so, the Christians at this time cannot, on the most favourable computation, have amounted to much more than $\frac{1}{150}$th of the whole human race; for the scanty congregations outside the limits of the Empire may be dismissed from our reckoning, as they would not appreciably affect the result. I am quite aware that the relative strength of Christendom at the two epochs is determined by other considerations as well as the numbers. But, after all deductions made on this account, shall we suffer ourselves to be overwhelmed with dismay because, as we pass from the third century to the nineteenth, the proportion of one in a hundred and fifty is only exchanged to one in five?

Soon after the epoch which I have chosen, the proportion doubtless was vastly increased.[1] The conversion of the Emperor had an enormous influence on the conversion of the Empire. Then the

[1] Yet even at the close of the fourth century St. Chrysostom, who certainly would not be likely to underrate their numbers, reckons the Christians of Antioch at 100,000 (vii. p. 810), while he states the whole population of the city to be 200,000 (ii. p. 597). Consistently with this he elsewhere (i. p. 592) speaks of the Christians as "the majority of the city" (τὸ πλέον τῆς πόλεως). Gibbon, overlooking the second passage, reckons the whole population of Antioch at "not less than half a million," so that the Christians would only form one-fifth of the whole, and endeavours to show that this estimate is consistent with the third passage. But whatever reasons there may be for taking this larger estimate of the population, it was clearly not St. Chrysostom's. Still the fact is striking enough that "after Christianity had enjoyed during more than sixty years the sunshine of Imperial favour," the Christians constituted only about half of the population in a city which had had greater advantages than any other.

L. E. G

barbarian tribes poured in, sweeping everything before them. They came, saw, and were conquered. Mohammedanism constrained the vanquished, but Christianity conquered the conqueror. Yet even then it is quite a mistake to suppose that wherever the banner of the Gospel was carried, the victory was rapid and complete. Take the case of our own island. There were Christians in Britain at all events before the end of the second century, when Tertullian wrote.[1] Yet four centuries later, when Augustine landed, he found the Christian communities feeble and insignificant—so feeble that they had done nothing towards evangelizing the Teutonic invaders, though a whole century had elapsed since their occupation of the island. And shall we then, with this lesson before us, hang our hands in despair because, after a little more than half a century of not too zealous missionary effort,[2] India is not already prostrate at the foot of the Cross? But let me pass from this comparison of proportions to some analogies between ancient and modern missions,

---

[1] Tertull. *adv. Jud.* c. 7, "Britannorum inaccessa Romanis loca."

[2] "Bearing in mind," wrote Lord Lawrence to the *Times*, 4th Jan. 1873, "that general missionary effort in India dates from 1813, and that even now missionaries are sent forth in such inadequate numbers that, with few exceptions, only the large towns and centres have been occupied (some of them with a single missionary), it was scarcely to be expected that in the course of sixty years the idols of India would be utterly abolished ; the wonder rather is that already there are so many unmistakable indications that Hinduism is fast losing its hold upon the affections of the people."

which also have their lessons of consolation and encouragement.

(1) When we look to the history of ancient missions, we find an enormous difference in the rates of progress with different religions and races. The rude and barbarous northern tribes seem to fall like full-ripe fruit before the first breath of the Gospel. The Goths and the Vandals who poured down upon the Roman Empire were evangelized so silently or so rapidly that only a fact here and there relating to their conversion has been preserved. At a later date the baptism of a prince carries with it the baptism of his people. Clovis among the Franks, Ethelbert in Kent, are instances of this. But wherever the Gospel found itself confronted with a high civilization and an old historic religion, the case was widely different. The religion of Rome was interwoven with its history, with its literature, with its institutions, with the whole texture of its domestic and political life. Against this mass of time-honoured custom and prestige the wave of the Gospel beat for centuries in vain. Slowly and gradually it was undermining the fabric, but no striking results were immediately visible. It is an established fact that the Roman Church for the first two centuries was not Latin. It was composed of Greeks and Orientals, who had made the metropolis their home. Its bishops were Greek, its language was Greek. More than half a centur after Constantine's conversion, it is, I think, plain that old

Latin Rome—the senate, the aristocracy, the cultivated and influential classes—was still in great part pagan, so far as it was anything. Not very dissimilar was the case of Athens. St. Paul, though eminently successful with the mixed and floating population of her neighbour Corinth, produced next to no immediate effect on this historic centre of Greek culture and religion, this stronghold of an ancient δεισιδαιμονία.

Now all this is exactly analogous to our modern experience in India. The success of our missions among the rude aboriginal or non-Aryan tribes is everywhere astonishing. Here alone is an enormous field for missionary enterprise; for these races are said to amount in the aggregate to not less than forty millions of people. I have heard it stated (and, so far as I can see, the statement is quite justified by past experience) that we have only to send fairly zealous missionaries among them in sufficient force, and their conversion in any numbers may be reckoned on almost as a matter of course. Only the other day I was shown a letter from the chief missionary station among the Kols. At a recent visit of the Bishop to this station there were not less than 250 communicants in one day, and 375 on the next—none the same as those who had communicated the day before. Are there many churches in England where such a muster as this could be found? On this same occasion five natives were ordained deacons and more than 250 confirmed; and in the last twelve months over 700 persons have been baptized, of whom more than 450 are converts from heathenism, with their children. The missionary triumphs among the ruder tribes in another part of India, in Tinnevelly, are well known. The number of native Christians there now amounts, I believe, to 50,000 or more. It increases quite as rapidly as, with the existing staff of teachers, we ought perhaps to desire. But with the Hindu proper the Gospel has hitherto made no progress which is very appreciable at a distance. Does history encourage us to expect any other result? Not in one generation, nor in two, nor perhaps in ten, will the victory be achieved. We must be prepared to labour and to wait. If our faith needs sustaining by immediate tangible results, we must look elsewhere for consolation—to the ruder tribes of India of whom I have just spoken; or to Sierra Leone, where at least seven-eighths of the people are now Christians, though the first mission does not date farther back than the present century; or to New Zealand, where the native population was converted almost within a single generation.

(2) But, again, it is a patent fact, becoming more patent every day, that though the educated Hindu does not readily embrace Christianity, yet his own religion is relaxing its hold upon him. The prominence given to this "disintegrating agency" of contact with Christianity is perhaps the most remarkable feature in Sir B. Frere's very remarkable

paper on Indian Missions. "Statistical facts," he says, "can in no way convey any adequate idea of the work done in any part of India. The effect is often enormous, where there has not been a single avowed conversion."[1] To some persons this negative result may not appear a very encouraging fact. Yet, read by the light of history, it is far from the reverse; for history teaches us to regard this as a natural, almost a necessary, stage of transition from an ancient historic religion to Christianity. It is the great shaking of the nation which, in the prophet's image, preludes the inpouring of its gifts to the temple of the Lord.[2] The cultivated classes among the Greeks and Romans passed through a period of deism or of scepticism, after the popular mythology had ceased to satisfy and before Christianity had secured its hold. The Brahma Somaj is not the first instance in the history of Christianity where a system too vague and shadowy and too deficient in the elements of a permanent religion has filled the interval between the abandonment of the old and the acceptance of the new.

(3) But we may carry our comparison a step

[1] *The Church and the Age*, p. 339. In a lecture delivered 9th July 1872, Sir B. Frere speaks even more strongly : "I assure you that, whatever you may be told to the contrary, the teaching of Christianity among 160 millions of civilised industrious Hindus and Mohammedans in India is effecting changes, moral, social, and political, which for extent and rapidity of effect are far more extraordinary than you or your fathers have witnessed in modern Europe." The testimony of Lord Lawrence, in the letter already quoted, is to the same effect.

[2] Haggai ii. 7.

farther. If ancient missionary history, like modern, has had its periods of slow and painful progress, the importance of such periods has been vindicated in the sequel. These epochs of patient working and waiting have been succeeded by magnificent and sudden triumphs—fitful and capricious, as we might be disposed to regard them. But is it not more reasonable to look upon these triumphs as the long-deferred fruit of painful labour which has been expended in tilling the ground? Thus, when very little seemed to be doing, as a matter of fact everything was doing. Such a time of preparation was the period preceding the date which I took as my starting-point, the middle of the third century of the Christian era. The missionaries in New Zealand worked on for several years without making a single convert, for full twenty years without producing any striking effect. All at once the aspect of things was changed, and within an incredibly short space of time more than half the Maori population became Christians. Can we suppose that there was no connexion between those long labours and that rapid triumph? Shall we believe that if Mr. Marsden had first visited New Zealand at the end of those twenty years, instead of the beginning, the result would have been quite the same? But let us apply this experience to our Indian Empire. We are still in the midst—perhaps not yet in the midst—of this probationary period; for where the aim is more magnificent, the effort also will be prolonged. But shall we throw away all the toil expended in preparing and watering the ground, because the plant has hardly yet appeared above the surface of the soil, and the harvest is still distant?

And indeed, though the progress has not been so rapid as our zeal or our impatience would demand, it has been distinct, and it has been steady. The decennial returns of Indian Missions for the years 1851, 1861, and 1871 have been placed in my hands. I find that the rate of increase is, roughly speaking, 50 per cent in each decennium. The numbers of native Christians, catechumens, and learners at these three dates are over 91,000, 138,000, and 224,000 respectively. Thus the numbers have considerably more than doubled in twenty years. This return does not include the independent States; neither does it include Burma, in which latter territory alone the numbers of native Christians at the end of the year 1861 amounted to nearly 60,000, the progress of the Burmese missions having been remarkably rapid. Moreover, these calculations do not comprise the Roman Catholic missions, of which I have no returns, and which doubtless would very largely swell the numbers. The totals in themselves, I venture to think, do not at all justify the disparaging language which we frequently hear; but the point on which I would especially lay stress is the *steadiness* of the increase.

For this steadiness is the most healthy sign. Where whole multitudes are suddenly converted without any previous preparation, the result is always precarious. What was the after history of those 500,000 whom St. Francis Xavier is said to have evangelized in the south in nine years, when the magic of his personal presence was withdrawn? Or of those 300,000 Singalese whom the Dutch in Ceylon had already converted at the close of the seventeenth century, when the Dutch supremacy was removed?

(4) Again, we hear much of the obstacles thrown in the way of missionary success by the divisions between Christian and Christian. We may indeed quote the high authority of Sir B. Frere for saying that this hindrance is much less on the spot than it appears at a distance. But let it be granted that we have here a most serious impediment to our progress. Was there nothing corresponding to it in the first ages of the Church? We need only recall the names of Ebionites, Basilideans, Ophites, Valentinians, Marcionites, and numberless other heretical sects—differing from each other and from the Catholic Church incomparably more widely in creed than the Baptist differs from the Romanist— to dispel this illusion at once. The sectarian divisions of the early Christians supply their heathen adversary Celsus with a capital argument against the claims of the Gospel and the Church. *Nos passi graviora.* We have surmounted worse obstacles than these of to-day.

(5) Lastly, whatever discouragements we may

have encountered in our English missions in this nineteenth century, they pale into insignificance before the unparalleled disasters which have overtaken the Church of Christ in the past, and from which nevertheless she has ever risen again to develop fresh energies and achieve higher victories. Shall we be disheartened if at one point the frontier of Christianity should seem to be receding rather than advancing, or if at another some tribe of converts should suddenly relapse into semi-heathenism? Let us remember how the once flourishing and populous Church of Africa, with its 600 or 700 bishoprics, dwindled away under the withering blast of the Donatist schism and the ruthless devastations of the Vandal invasion, till at length the inpouring tide of Mohammedanism overwhelmed the land and swept away the last traces of its existence. Or, if we would console ourselves with an example on a yet grander scale, we may place ourselves in imagination in the middle of the tenth century, and survey the scene of desolation which meets the eye on every side. I can compare the condition of the Church at this epoch to nothing else but the fate of the prisoner in the story as he awakens to the fact that the walls of his iron den are closing in upon him, and shudders to think of the inevitable end. For on all sides the heathen and the infidel were tightening their grip upon Christendom. On the north and west, the pagan Scandinavians hanging about every coast and pouring in at every inlet;

on the east, the pagan Hungarians swarming like locusts and devastating Europe from the Baltic to the Alps; on the south and south-east, the infidel Saracens pressing on and on with their victorious hosts—it seemed as if every pore of life were choked, and Christendom must be stifled and smothered in the fatal embrace. But Christendom revived, flourished, spread. How, then, shall we suffer a petty disappointment here or there in the wide field of missionary enterprise to dishearten and to paralyse us, where there is so much to cheer and to stimulate? Again I say, *Nos passi graviora*. We have survived worse calamities than these.

In this comparison of the present with the past, I have attempted to show that the missions of the nineteenth century are in no sense a failure. But I seem to see the advent of a more glorious future, if we will only nerve ourselves to renewed efforts. During the past half-century we have only been learning our work, as a missionary Church. At length experience is beginning to tell. India is our special charge, as a Christian nation; India is our hardest problem, as a missionary Church. Hitherto we have kept too exclusively to beaten paths. Our mode of dealing with the Indian has been too conventional, too English. Indian Christianity can never be cast in the same mould as English Christianity. We must make up our minds to this. The stamp of teaching, the mode of life, which experience has justified as the best possible for an English parish, may be very unfit when transplanted into an Indian soil. We must become as Indians to the Indian, if we would win India to Christ. This lesson of the past I find frankly recognized and courageously avowed from at least two distinct quarters of the Indian Mission field quite recently—in the stirring appeal which the Bishop of Bombay has addressed to the English Church through our Archbishop, and in those noble letters from Lahore, so zealous, so thoughtful, and so bold, which Mr. French has written to the Church Missionary Society. This coincidence, representing, as I doubt not, a much wider feeling, is surely full of hope for the future.

ENGLAND DURING THE LATTER HALF OF THE THIRTEENTH CENTURY

I

THE title of these lectures, as announced, is England and the English in the Thirteenth Century. On looking at the syllabus, however, you will see that the illustrations are drawn almost entirely from the latter half of the century. To this period I propose confining myself—to the later years of Henry III., which were occupied in the conflict between the King and the Barons, and to the reign of Edward I., when the principles asserted in that conflict were developed and matured. These limits will not be transgressed on either side, except so far as it may be necessary to explain the career of men, or the development of principles, or the progress of events, by reference to what had gone before or to what was coming after. The last fifty years comprise, at least as regards England, almost all that is greatest in the characteristics, movements, and the heroic personages of the century.

And certainly, if the lectures lack interest, the fault will lie not in the theme, but in the lecturer. We need only recall a few of the principal names which throw a glory on the annals of this period to assure ourselves of its unrivalled magnificence. At no other epoch in the mediæval or modern history of Europe, until we reach the great religious and intellectual movement of the sixteenth century opening out into

"The spacious times of great Elizabeth,"

do we meet with so brilliant a roll of famous men, living at or about the same time—great sovereigns, great statesmen, great lawyers, great men of science, great philosophers and divines, great architects, great poets and painters. Need I remind you that Edward, the ablest and greatest of English kings since the Conquest, was the godson and companion-in-arms of the best, perhaps the greatest, in the long line of French kings, Louis IX.; that in early boyhood he had been a contemporary of the brilliant, chivalrous, despotic, daring Frederick II., the wonder of the world, as he was called, the last and ablest Emperor of the illustrious House of Hohenstaufen; and through a large part of his life was the contemporary of the upright, wise, far-seeing Rudolph, the founder of a long line of powerful sovereigns, the first and perhaps the most famous Emperor of the famous House of Hapsburg? Need I say that in early manhood he fleshed his virgin sword in conflict with the great Simon de Montfort, the pioneer of English statesmanship, and that in later life he again unsheathed it against the famous William Wallace, the champion of Scottish independence? Need I recall the fact that not long after Edward ascended the throne died the famous doctor, Thomas of Aquinum; and apparently in the very same year was born the hardly less famous doctor, Duns Scotus; and again, that the great antagonist of Duns Scotus, William of Occam, was already rising into fame before the close of this reign; so that the foundations of the two great controversies which divided the empire of mediæval thought for many generations—the rivalry of Thomists and Scotists, and the rivalry of Realists and Nominalists—were laid under Edward's own eyes, and in Edward's own realm? Need I say that some years before his death the greatest of all modern poets—with one single exception—Dante, the father of European poetry—already, as he himself expresses it, in the midpath of his life, lost his way in that dark mysterious wood which led him to his awful, solemn, dazzling, beatific vision —at once the most magnificent of poems and the most impressive of sermons? Or need I add that at this same time already the shepherd boy, found accidentally by Cimabué in the neighbourhood of Florence

"Tracing his idle fancies on the ground,"

had quite eclipsed his master's fame, and the cry was

all for Giotto, Giotto, the great reformer of his art, the true founder of the most magnificent school of painting which the world has ever seen? Or need I remark that Edward numbered among his own subjects the greatest scientific name of mediæval times, Roger Bacon, whose intellectual penetration and inventive genius were only equalled by his encyclopædic knowledge, and whose foresight, "dipping into the future" and seeing

"The vision of the world and all the glory that should be,"

told by anticipation those "fairy tales of science" which to his own generation and for many centuries after must have seemed only the idle fancies of an enthusiastic dreamer, but which modern invention has vindicated as the very words of solemnness and truth? Or, if these names are insufficient, shall I go on to enrich the list with others, whose lustre indeed has been dulled by the breath of time, but who exercised, nevertheless, a spell of transcendent power over the minds of their own and succeeding generations, men like Albertus Magnus and Alexander of Hales, and Raymond Lully and Bonaventura—the Coleridges, and the Mills, and the Maurices, and the Carlyles of their day?

But I must not travel too far. With an almost limitless subject and a comparatively limited time allowed for its treatment, I must confine myself strictly to England. It would be interesting, indeed, to dwell upon the contemporary movements of political and intellectual life on the Continent; it would not be unprofitable to cast a glance at the synchronous history of the farther East, and to trace the astonishing progress of those Mongolian hordes whose ascendency was to exercise so powerful an influence on the destinies of Europe and the world; but England is our proper subject. And for England this era has a special importance. It is the real birth-time of the England of to-day. In this respect at least it exceeds in significance any later epoch in our national history.

"Then it was," writes Lord Macaulay in his splendid summary, "that the great English people was formed, that the national character began to exhibit those peculiarities which it has ever since retained, and that our fathers became emphatically islanders —islanders not merely in geographical position, but in their politics, their feelings, and their manners. Then first appeared with distinctness that constitution which has ever since, through all changes, preserved its identity; that constitution of which all the other free constitutions in the world are copies, and which, in spite of some defects, deserves to be regarded as the best under which any great society has ever existed during many ages. Then it was that the House of Commons, the archetype of all the representative assemblies which now meet, either in the old or in the new world, held its first sittings. Then it was that the common law rose to the dignity of a science, and rapidly became a not unworthy rival of the imperial jurisprudence. Then it was that the courage of those sailors who manned the rude barks of the Cinque Ports first made the flag of England terrible on the seas. Then it was that the most ancient colleges which still exist at both the great national seats of learning were founded. Then was formed that language, less musical indeed than the languages of the South, but in force, in richness, in aptitude for all the highest purposes of the poet, the philosopher, and the orator, inferior to the Greek tongue alone. Then, too, appeared the first faint dawn of that noble literature, the most splendid and the most durable of the many glories of England."

In this glowing panegyric on the thirteenth century Lord Macaulay has certainly not erred on the side of exaggeration. There are, indeed, two remarkable omissions in his summary, which ought not to be passed over in silence. In enumerating the rich gifts which this century bestowed on England, and through England on the world, it was surely a strange oversight to say nothing of the remarkable development in architecture, which, I venture boldly to say, with one exception, and that a doubtful exception, stands alone in the history of the world. The age of Pericles is the only possible architectural rival of the age of Edward I.

And again, the day is past when the student of history might have satisfied himself with dismissing the scholastic philosophy with a self-complacent sarcasm or a scornful silence, as an altogether foolish and exploded thing. This might have been tolerated a generation or two ago ; but we have been taught —your own Sir W. Hamilton has taught us—how largely modern philosophical speculation is indebted to the issues raised and the terms defined by these mediæval thinkers. We have found out—it is strange that we were so long in finding out—how widely even our popular language is impregnated with the distinctions of the schoolmen. But England bore a chief part—I might almost say the chief part —in the controversies of scholasticism. No review of England in the thirteenth century would be complete which failed to take this element into account.

These two points, however—the architecture and the scholasticism of England at this period—belong properly to my second lecture. I only mention them here, lest I should seem to pass over such grave omissions in this otherwise admirable summary.

To those, however, whose standard of valuation is purely arithmetical, it must be confessed that England in the thirteenth century will cut a very poor figure indeed. If an overgrown population or a bloated revenue is the true test of greatness, then the England of this time was anything but great. Its population amounted, according to the highest estimate, to some two millions and a half ; according to a lower and perhaps more probable estimate, to not much over one million and a half. Thus on any showing it was considerably less than the present population of London alone; while if the lower estimate be correct, it did not amount to half that number. Again, the metropolis itself is reckoned according to various statisticians to have contained from twenty to forty thousand human beings. Even if we adopt the largest estimate, it still falls far short of the *annual* increase in the population of London at the present day. The second city in the kingdom was Winchester. Its population is reckoned at ten thousand. Among the towns next in importance were York and Lincoln, Norwich and Northampton, the two latter famous for their manufactures, together with such seaports as Newcastle and Yarmouth, Dover and Southampton.

And again, when we read that the revenue in the last year of this thirteenth century did not reach £60,000, we must hang our heads in shame to think how contemptible the England of that day must appear to a Chancellor of the Exchequer in our own time who shows a proper scorn for low figures whether in the coffers of the State or on the plain of Marathon.

Yet, notwithstanding its small population and meagre revenue, this was the England which rose to the first position in the commonwealth of nations, which by force of arms inspired such terror and commanded such respect throughout Europe as it has never inspired and commanded since, and which in continental politics attained an influence never afterwards surpassed, and only equalled—if even then it was equalled—many centuries later in the struggle with the first Napoleon.

And again, if our only idea of civilization is the diffusion of material comforts and the growth of luxurious refinement, we shall be forced to confess that the subjects of Henry III. and Edward I. were sunk low in the depths of barbarism. So far as I can make out, England was in these respects far behind France and Italy and Spain. Picture to yourself the dining-hall in the ordinary manor-house of England at this time. The windows are not glazed, but closed by wooden shutters; consequently they are placed high up that the draught of cold may not be excessive. Window glass is still a novelty, confined, for the most part, to the palaces of the king and the mansions of the nobles, and even here used sparingly. It is all imported from abroad. Nearly two centuries must yet elapse before window glass is manufactured in England itself. The floor is most probably the natural soil, rammed down and perhaps strewn with rushes. If the owner is exceptionally well off it may be boarded, at least at the upper end. Not improbably there will be an open gutter running along the room, as we know was the case even in the Great Hall at Westminster, into which the refuse and dirty water was poured. The lower part of the room is apt to get sloppy. There will be a pool of water or a layer of green mould; hence the space below the dais is sometimes called the "marsh." The furniture is as rude as you might expect in such a room. The tables consist of boards resting on trestles; they are removed when the meal is over and tilted up against the walls. The guests sit on forms covered with mats. The dinner service accords with the furniture. It consists of flat wooden, or occasionally pewter, trenchers, a few wooden bowls, two or three brass dishes, and some knives and spoons. Fingers are still in requisition, for forks are a refinement unknown except at the table of the king. The meat is handed round on spits after the fashion of a Homeric feast—this is the case even at royal banquets—and each person cuts off from the joint what he pleases. Of the viands themselves some curious notices are preserved. In the household accounts of the king's sister, the Countess of Leicester, are items for whale's flesh and porpoise. Yet these, our rude forefathers, were the men who designed and erected the glories of Lincoln and Westminster, the stately grace of the Chapter House at Salisbury, and the chaste magnificence of the Choir at Ely—who studded England over with consummate works of art, of which we, attempting a vain rivalry, produce only slavish copies or stiff and clumsy caricatures.

> " Privatus illis census erat brevis,
> Commune magnum :
>
> Nec fortuitum spernere cæspitem
> Leges sinebant, oppida publico
> Sumptu jubentes et deorum
> Templa novo decorare saxo."

But great as were the achievements of this thirteenth century, its promises were still greater than its performances. Mr. Stubbs, in one of those pregnant summaries prefixed to the several chapters in his collection of documents, describes it as a *precocious* age. No epithet could be more admirably chosen. In this *precocity* you have the explanation of its failures. It was, in fact, at least two or three centuries before its time. The proper sequel to the thirteenth century is the sixteenth. In Edward's reign England seems ripe, or at least ripening, for that rich harvest which was only gathered under the later Tudors and the earlier Stuarts. Why did the revival of Greek learning under Grossteste come to nothing? Why did Roger Bacon's conceptions of a true theology, founded on Biblical exegesis, wait to be realized by Erasmus and Luther and Calvin, and his principles of the true scientific method, founded on experiment, lie barren till they were taken up by his great namesake under James I.? Why did Edward's project of a united British Empire remain unfulfilled till, three centuries later, the force of circumstances placed a Scottish prince on the throne of England? We can only say that all these ideas were premature. The thirteenth century had outgrown its strength. It was succeeded by the hollow parade of the fourteenth century, which bore much flower but no fruit; which, with a dazzling show of achievement, really achieved nothing. Then followed the degradation of the fifteenth century. And then at length the long-deferred season came.

The thirteenth century had been stimulated into excessive, because premature, activity, intellectual and political. If we ask for the cause of this remarkable phenomenon, the reply is to be found in the Crusades. King Edward I., the representative sovereign of this great age, was (we should bear it in mind) the last Crusader of the last Crusade. We are too apt to look upon the Crusades as gigantic frauds on humanity—splendid delusions, it may be, but delusions from beginning to end. In their immediate purpose, indeed, they were an entire failure, as they deserved to be. But there is always something magnificent in a great enthusiasm; and such an enthusiasm can never be fruitless. The Crusades, in fact, were the great educators of mediæval Europe. Like the young man who takes a time of foreign travel before settling down to the hard business of life, all Europe had gone abroad, as it were, and, having worked off the crude passions of its rising youth, now returned home with enlarged experience, with extended knowledge, with new ideas and quickened energy.

About two centuries had elapsed since the Norman Conquest, when the Barons' War broke out—a period of time, be it remembered, as long as that which separates us from the Restoration. I mention this because we do not without an effort realize distances in the remote past where the long perspective of time diminishes and foreshortens the intervals. And certainly the England of the later years of Henry

III. was quite as unlike the England of William I., as the England of Victoria is unlike the England of Charles II. The great work of these two centuries had been the amalgamation of the Norman and the English. The descendants of the great feudal lords, who had come over with the Conqueror or been introduced by his immediate successors, were as thoroughly English in all their sympathies and feelings, as the veriest Saxon gentleman whose ancestors had lived from time immemorial on the soil. They had slowly imbibed all those insular interests and prejudices, which have been at once the strength and the weakness of the Englishman in every age. The French favourites of Henry III. were equally foreigners, equally hateful to these Norman Englishmen as to those Saxon Englishmen. And indeed the amalgamation was only natural. If it be true that blood is thicker than water, then the descendant of the hardy Norseman, despite his settlement on French soil, his acquisition of the French language, and his veneer of French civilization, must naturally have been more at home with the Teutonic native of England than with the Celto-Romanic intruder from the Continent. "In the time of Richard the First," says Lord Macaulay, "the ordinary imprecation of a Norman gentleman was 'May I become an Englishman.' His ordinary form of indignant denial was 'Do you take me for an Englishman?' The descendant of such a gentleman a hundred years later was proud of the English name."

The leaven, indeed, had been long working; but for the consummation of the change England is indebted, not to the virtues but to the vices of two sovereigns—to the wickedness of John and the weakness of Henry III. When Edward I. ascended the throne, England was no longer Anglo-Norman, but English. For this inestimable blessing, however, she owed no thanks either to his father or to his grandfather. To Edward himself, an Englishman to the core, who recognized this fact and worked it out in all its bearings, her debt of gratitude is almost incalculable.

"The follies and vices" of John, says Lord Macaulay, "were the salvation" of England. And in the same spirit Mr. Freeman contrasts France, which suffered from "the baleful virtues of the most righteous of kings, St. Lewis," and England, where "we had the momentary curse, the lasting blessing, of a succession of evil kings." Certainly out of the baseness, the profligacy, the recklessness of the worst of her sovereigns, England carved two substantial benefits.

The loss of Normandy was the eternal disgrace of John. It was nothing less than the making of England. The grave perplexities in which the possession of Hanover involved us during the great European wars of the last century, the still more serious embroilments in which we should have found ourselves if it had still continued attached to the English Crown during the Prusso-Austrian war of 1866, or the Franco-German war of 1870-71, will only enable us very faintly to realize the encumbrance of Normandy to England in the twelfth and thirteenth centuries. For our sovereigns were dukes of Normandy before they were kings of England; and this fact England was never allowed to forget. England existed for the sake of Normandy. Of some of her kings England saw next to nothing. Their time was spent in Normandy, when they were not engaged in more distant wars. Richard I. reigned ten years: he did not pass as many months in England. The cutting adrift of Normandy was the first and the most important step towards the consolidation of England as England.

This blessing, affecting her *external* relations, she owed to the reckless trifling of John. The second, which affected her *internal* constitution, was wrested from his profligacy and baseness. Nothing short of monstrous and almost preterhuman wickedness could have leagued together all classes, Normans and English, barons and clergy and people, against the sovereign, for the assertion of the national rights in *Magna Charta*. *Magna Charta* did not contain any novelty. It was a mere repetition of rights which singly had been claimed and conceded before; but it brought together into one focus all the points for which the champions of national freedom had contended; it placed on record the principles which were to govern England for the future; it pledged the sovereign solemnly to the maintenance of these principles; and it formed a rallying-point round which after generations could gather. This was its most obvious gain. But its secondary and indirect effect was not less momentous. By the spirit which the struggle evoked, it had conduced most materially to the unification of England. Thus it carried on the work which the loss of Normandy had begun.

John died in 1216. Then succeeded a long reign of fifty-six years—the longest on record, with one recent exception, in the annals of our English kings.

Of the character of Henry III. little need be said. He was feeble, capricious, petulant, ready to promise and quick to forget his promise, "unstable as water" like the patriarch of old, and like him destined not to excel. A contemporary chronicler speaks of the "waxen" heart of the king. He had some of the passion, but none of the energy and courage of his race. Like his forefathers he could say strong things, but, unlike them, he could not do strong deeds. He was intensely religious, in his own way; but his piety was not of a manly sort. The great Italian poet gives him a place in purgatory among the useless and simple folk "not for doing, but for not doing." "Our English Nestor," says old Fuller, "not for depth of brains, but for length of life;" adding, "All the months in a year may in a manner be carried out of an April day, hot, cold, dry, moist, fair, foul weather being oft presented therein. Such the character of this king's life, certain only in uncertainty, sorrowful, successful, in plenty, in penury, in wealth, in want, conquered, conqueror."

It is with the later and most chequered years of this long and chequered reign that I am mainly concerned, the period comprising the Barons' War. For then it was that the weakness of Henry consummated for England the great work which the vices of John had begun. Now, as before, this work is twofold. It is, *first*, the recognition of England as England, and, *secondly*, the development of constitutional liberty.

The one fault in Henry's administration which his subjects could least forgive was his partiality for foreigners. It might have appeared that circumstances had combined to make him thoroughly English; and yet he resisted circumstances. Owing to his father's loss of his continental possessions, Henry was the first sovereign of England since the Conquest who had been born on English soil. And yet all the chief dignities in Church and State, even the inferior offices about the Court, were lavished on strangers. Two swarms of these foreign locusts more especially preyed upon the resources of England—the relations of his wife, Eleanor of Provence, and his own half brothers and sisters, the sons and daughters of his mother Isabella, with their hangers-on. Two or three generations before this might have been borne with patience. But the English spirit, after its long eclipse, had revived; and these swarms of foreign locusts were intolerable to all classes alike. England must be cleared of this brood of ungodly curs (so a political song of the time styles them) which were preying on her vitals.

Moreover, a struggle had now been going on for some years between the king and his subjects about the maintenance of the Great Charter. Again and again Henry had renewed his pledge to observe its provisions, and again and again he had recklessly violated his oath. He had persuaded himself that no faith need be kept between a king and his subjects; that, as the latter had no right to extort a pledge, so the former was not bound to observe it. It was clear that matters had come to a crisis. The knot of the political situation could no longer be untied by peaceful methods: it must be cut by the sword.

Hence the struggle, which is commonly, though not very correctly, called the Barons' War. It was the war of constitutional liberty, in which, thanks to the wickedness of John and the treachery of Henry, the barons had ranged themselves on the popular side. And the two points at issue in the contest were the same two which had been involved in the troubles of John's reign. The double war-cry of the national party was "England for the English" and the "maintenance of the Charters."

The struggle presents some curious coincidences with another civil war four centuries later, when again the liberties of England were at stake. When we read the account of the night preceding the battle of Lewes—of the revelry and riot of the royalist forces, of the solemn exhortations to repentance and prayer in the national army—we are forcibly reminded of the attitude of Cavaliers and Puritans in the great Parliamentary war of the seventeenth century. The manifestoes of the Baronial party have, as we shall see, a strongly Puritan tinge. The Puritan preachers of the thirteenth century were the Franciscan friars. The comparison may seem paradoxical at first sight—we are accustomed to regard the two as the opposite poles of religious life—but it is, I believe, perfectly just. The shaven crown and bare feet of the one, the straight hair and sober-coloured suit of the other, are only accidents. The spirit is the same. The Franciscans thoroughly identified themselves with the national party. Simon de Montfort had been the intimate friend of Adam de Marisco, and of Bishop Grossteste, the one the leader, and the other the patron, of the English Franciscans. The Franciscans (there is reason to think) wrote their political ballads for the barons. They were the earnest fanatical preachers of their day, the dreaded opponents of the parochial clergy, and the great innovators upon the traditional usages of the Church.

And in another point, too, the parallel between the two movements, though separated by an interval of four centuries, is striking. The strength of the national party in both cases is drawn very much from the same localities. In both struggles the citizens of London take their side against the king.

Liberty with them has ever been a more powerful sentiment than loyalty. In both the national armies are recruited and officered very largely from the eastern counties.

In this struggle one figure towers far above the rest in moral and intellectual stature, and may fitly claim to rank among the greatest men of any age. The national cause had found an ally in the most unexpected quarter. The principles at stake were purely and essentially *English*, and yet the leader was no Englishman.

> "Via prima salutis,
> Quod minime reris, Graia pandetur ab urbe."

Simon de Montfort, the champion of English liberties, the founder, so far as any one man can be regarded the founder, of the English House of Commons, was a Frenchman by birth and descent. But he had inherited the important earldom of Leicester, and thus he came to reside in England. His relations with the king, whose sister he had married, were variable and uncertain, as might have been expected from Henry's instability of character; but into the affections of the English people he was entwining himself more closely day by day. He was admirably fitted for a popular hero. He was a brave soldier and a consummate general; he was steadfast and resolute in his purpose, not deterred by any wailing nor shaken by any defeat. He was a wise and large-minded statesman, as he showed when the counsels of war gave way to the counsels of peace. He had a lofty spirit, which soared far above all base considerations of personal interest. In short, he was essentially a true man. Moreover, he had a manly and robust piety, which he did not think it necessary to hide, and which, not less than his courage and ability, won for him the instinctive respect of the English people. To his contemporaries he seemed not more a hero than a saint.

At the moment at which we have arrived the extravagance and mismanagement of the king have brought matters to a crisis. By the strong remonstrances of Simon de Montfort he has been obliged to summon a Great Council to consider the condition of the kingdom. The Council met at Oxford in June 1258. This Council has sometimes been called by later historians the "Mad Parliament," but certainly there was method—and a wise method too—in its madness. The barons and their party mustered in great force. The general discontent of the kingdom had been heightened by an extraordinary famine. It was no longer possible for the king to refuse redress. The Council passed and the king consented to the provisions which were called the *Oxford Statutes*. In these *Magna Charta* was once more confirmed. And it was further provided that the offices and the fortresses, which were now in the hands of foreigners, should be delivered over to Englishmen.

When it came to the point, the king's foreign

114 ENGLAND DURING THE LATTER HALF

relations refused to surrender the castles which were in their hands. And here the true nobility of De Montfort's character shone forth. He, too, was a foreigner—bound equally with them by the conditions. He declared that he looked upon his oath as a solemn pledge, which under no circumstances he would break, whatever others might do. He therefore at once delivered up the fortresses which he held. Thus by his true honesty he forced his opponents to yield. All the castles were handed over to Englishmen; and the foreigners, seeing that there was now no place for them in England, for the most part forsook her shores.

It was significant of the change that the proclamation announcing the Oxford Statutes was published in *English*—this being the first time (so far as we know) that the English language was used in any State document since the Conquest (though nearly two hundred years had elapsed). Thus the whole English people were informed that England was herself once more, and that the battle of England's liberties had been won.

It was a bitter trial to King Henry to lose his foreign favourites and to forfeit his license of misgovernment. A loftier spirit would have accepted the position as inevitable; a more honourable man would have felt himself pledged by his oath. But Henry had no such scruples. He applied to the Pope to grant him a dispensation from his oath, on the ground that it had been extorted by undue pressure; and this dispensation the Pope granted. He began at once by fraud or by force to violate the conditions of the Oxford Statutes.

Hitherto the revolution had been bloodless. The liberties of England had been won in the council-chamber and not on the battle-field. For nearly fifty years the country had enjoyed immunity from civil war. In our own days in England, happily, we do not know what civil war means. The respect of sovereign and parliament and people for the *law* and the *constitution* has saved us (as may it long save us!) from this most terrible of all scourges. But in those times, when the Norman and English elements in the nation were not completely fused and harmonized, when the liberties of the subject were not strictly guarded, and the constitution itself was yet a matter of contention, a half-century was an exceptionally long period to pass without the sword being unsheathed in some contest between Englishmen and Englishmen, and without the consequent desolation of English hearths and homes by English hands. It is only as a last resource that civil war can under any circumstances be justified; only, when all other methods have failed, that a breach of the law is necessary to enforce the law. But now the time seemed to have come. The king's word could not be trusted. The appeal to arms was inevitable.

I will not trouble you with the earlier incidents of the struggle. It is sufficient to say that after some desultory warfare the barons in an evil hour consented to refer the dispute to the arbitration of the French king. His award was unfavourable to them. He annulled the Oxford Statutes; and he directed that the king should be free to commit the castles to whomsoever he desired. But, on the other hand, he declared that all the privileges, charters, and liberties which existed before the Oxford Statutes should continue in force.

This last provision did not satisfy the national party. They declared that it had been obtained by undue influences, and they refused to accept it. The war broke out anew. But the refusal to abide by the award alienated some of the leading barons, and strengthened the cause of the royalists. The national party had thus put themselves in the wrong. They had condescended to imitate the bad faith of the king; they had surrendered the lofty vantage-ground of honour, which hitherto they had strictly held; and they felt the consequences at once. Then it was, amid the desertion which ensued, that Earl Simon showed his stern, unbending, iron will, declaring, "Though all should leave me, yet with my four sons I will stand true to the just cause which I have sworn to uphold for the honour of the Church and the benefit of the kingdom."

At the first renewal of hostilities the royalists gained some successes. But their triumph was short-lived. The award had been given in January 1264. In May of the same year the royalist army was gathered a few miles from the South coast, at Lewes. Their headquarters were at the Priory. Here were gathered together King Henry and his brother Richard, King of the Romans, with the two princes, Edward, the eldest son of Henry, and Henry, the eldest son of Richard. Meanwhile, Simon de Montfort's army was advancing upon them from the north.

We are now on the eve of the great battle of *Lewes*, ever memorable in our annals, for on its issue was staked the constitutional liberty of England.

The few intervening hours were passed in very different ways by the two armies which were so soon to engage. The royalist forces spent the night in revelry and riot. Even the sacred character of the place did not restrain them. The very altars of the church, it is reported, were profaned by gross debauchery. Meanwhile in the opposing army a solemn earnestness prevailed. Earl Simon committed himself and his cause to the protection of heaven, exhorting his soldiers to repent. They all put on the white cross, to show that they regarded themselves as fighting in a holy cause.

The town of Lewes lies underneath a range of those hills which are called the Downs, close to their south-eastern slopes. Over these hills marched the baronial army from the north-west. Thus they were hidden from view till they reached within a short distance of town. Then, when the bell tower of the Priory, which formed the headquarters of the king's army, came in view, Simon dismounted and once again summoned his army to prayer: "If we are God's, to God we commend our body and soul." The appeal was answered. The soldiers fell on their faces on the turf and prayed for victory.

As we approach Lewes the ridge of the hills branches out into three tongues, each separated from the other by intervening valleys, and all sloping down more or less gradually towards the town. This suggested to De Montfort the disposition of his forces. He divided his army into four. Three of these divisions were to advance towards Lewes along the three declivities; the fourth was posted as a reserve on the ridge under his own command.

Prince Edward commanded the right of the royalist army. He was opposed to the Londoners, who occupied the enemy's left. We may suppose that he chose this position purposely. Some time before a London mob had grossly insulted his mother, Queen Eleanor, as she left the Tower, which was then a royal residence, and put off in her barge for Windsor. This insult the high-spirited prince had never forgiven. And now, when the moment of vengeance had arrived, we may well suppose that he was eager not to let it slip.

Fiery, passionate, intent upon vengeance, reckless of consequences, Prince Edward, with the flower of the army, charged against the Londoners. Against such soldiers, led by such a leader, they were wholly unable to hold their ground. Their opponents were clad in mail and armed to the teeth; they themselves, half citizens, half soldiers, were ill equipped and ill disciplined. Against such odds even the staunchest courage was powerless. Along the slope of the Downs, over the perilous sides, across the plain they fled, pursued, trampled down, massacred, by the hot-blooded prince. Far away from Lewes, far away from the main scene of conflict, the pursuit was continued. For four long miles the ground was strewn with arms of the fugitives and the corpses of the slain, as the citizen troops retreated before his impetuous onset.

But blind passion seldom escapes its punishment, and the prince had bitter reason to rue his reckless thirst for vengeance. The cool eye of Simon de Montfort had seized the opportune moment. While Edward was far in the rear, smiting the hated Londoners hip and thigh, the Earl directed a firm steady blow against the royalist army weakened by the withdrawal of the prince's forces. Reinforcing his right with his own reserves, he attacked the enemy's centre and left, where the two kings were stationed, desiring, if possible, to gain possession of King Henry's person. The attack was successful. King Henry was driven back to his headquarters in the Priory; the King of the Romans took refuge in a mill, where he was blockaded and assailed with taunting gibes. "Come down, thou vile miller, thou forsooth to turn mill-master, thou that art satisfied with no meaner title than King of the Romans." Prince Richard had purchased this foreign title—

which his brother's English subjects turned to ridicule—with his enormous wealth.

The King of the Romans had already surrendered, the King of England was besieged in the Priory, when Prince Edward returned from his hot and reckless chase to find that all was over. His impetuosity had lost the day. Nothing remained but to capitulate. The two kings, with the princes, their sons, fell into the hands of Simon de Montfort.

His ascendency was not long-lived. The battle of Lewes, which made him master of the person of the king and the administration of the realm, was fought on the 14th of May 1264; the battle of Evesham, in which he was defeated and slain, on the 4th of August 1265. But during these fifteen months he was supreme. He assumed the protectorate of the realm. He was nominally the king's chief counsellor; practically his head gaoler. The royal policy was dictated by him; the royal manifestoes were composed by him.

And in this memorable interval was completed the framework of our parliamentary constitution. It was on the 24th of December 1264 that a summons was issued in the king's name for a parliament to meet in January. Parliaments, indeed, were no novelty; but they had been composed hitherto chiefly of barons and prelates, while on rare occasions knights of the shire had been invited. But now, for the first time, the representation of the boroughs was recognized. The cities and towns were directed "each to choose and send two discreet, loyal, and honest men"—so ran the writ—to the Great Council of the nation. We can hardly suppose that Earl Simon foresaw all the mighty consequences which would flow from this innovation. He could not have anticipated that this part of our representative system would, in course of time, far outstrip all others in importance. But it was one of those ventures of a generous patriotism which, by reason of their very generosity, bear fruit far beyond expectation. He saw that the town populations were growing in power and influence; and with a wise liberality he determined to give them a substantial voice in the national councils—a signal proof that he was no ambitious intriguer, bent on aggrandizement of his order or the advancement of himself at the expense of the royal prerogative, but a true-hearted champion of the national liberties.

The great Earl's power, however, was, as I have said, short-lived. The end was at hand. Hitherto Prince Edward had been kept under strict guard, practically, though not nominally, a captive. His escape was the turning-point in the fortunes of the two parties. The stratagem by which he effected it is well known. Pretending to try the speed of a new horse which had been given him against the other horses of his escort, he rode the rest in succession until he had utterly exhausted them; then mounting his own fresh steed he galloped him off at full speed, the jaded condition of the others having made pursuit impossible. He was soon beyond the reach of his enemies, and in friendly protection. This took place on the 28th of May.

The genius and energy of Prince Edward, thus set at liberty, quickly retrieved the fortunes of the royalists. I must pass over all the minor events of the next few months, and come to the time when the battle of Lewes was avenged by the battle of Evesham.

It was now the beginning of August. A son of the great Earl, who bore his father's name, Simon, was at Kenilworth, the hereditary castle of the Earl of Leicester, commanding a portion of the baronial army. An unworthy son of his father, the younger Simon was, so far as we can make out, a mere reckless, lawless, riotous soldier. At all events no effective discipline was maintained in his army; the soldiers spent their time in revelry and riot; they slept not within the fortifications of the castle, but in the open town outside its walls; and they kept no guard. Prince Edward, through his spies, obtained information of this state of things. Marching all night from Worcester, he arrived at Kenilworth at daybreak on the 2nd of August, and fell suddenly upon them, surprising them while still in their beds, capturing the whole force with the exception of a handful of fugitives who fled naked or half-dressed (among them young Simon de Montfort), and enriching his followers with their spoils.

Meanwhile the Earl himself, ignorant of the disaster which had befallen his son, reached Evesham with the king. This was on the morning of the 4th of August. Every moment was precious, for Prince Edward was suspected to be in the neighbourhood. But the king insisted on staying to breakfast there, and De Montfort had no choice but to yield. The delay was fatal.

The river Avon runs round the town of Evesham in a horse-shoe shape, almost enclosing it in its embrace, and leaving only a narrow outlet towards the north. Facing this outlet the ground slopes down southward towards the town in a succession of irregular waving hills. No more desperate position could be conceived for an army, outnumbered by the enemy, than to be thus locked in the folds of the river, without any chance of escape in case of defeat. On the other hand, a superior force, attacking from the north, would have everything in its favour, the slope of the ground, the course of the river, the inextricable position of the enemy.

As De Montfort was preparing to leave Evesham, a large army was descried on the hill-tops advancing towards the town from the north. It was a glad sight to him, for he thought that he saw the forces of his son. But to make sure, his barber, keen of sight and skilled in heraldry, was sent to the top of the Abbey tower to reconnoitre. Thence he saw emblazoned on the banners of the advancing hosts the three leopards, the badge of Prince Edward—the same three leopards which, transformed, I know not how and when, into lions, are still quartered on the Royal Arms of England. There could be no mistake. This was no friendly force, but the terrible prince himself at the head of the royalist army. "The Lord have mercy on our souls," cried Simon, when he was told the sad truth; "for our bodies are the enemy's."

Then the Earl's son Henry urged his father to escape, offering to face the battle alone. The brave old warrior refused. He had grown old in battle; let his son rather retire who was still in the flower of youth. But the son was steadfast as the father, and both together prepared to meet death.

It was a massacre rather than a battle. From the very first the Earl had seen that they had no chance. The bravest and noblest of the barons fell. Simon himself and his son Henry were slain. To the eternal disgrace of the royalists Simon's body was shamefully mutilated, and his head, horribly garnished, sent as a present to the wife of Roger de Mortimer, one of the royalist chieftains. Of all this, however, Prince Edward was guiltless. With true chivalrous spirit he bore his cousin, Henry de Montfort, to an honoured grave.

The victory of De Montfort at Lewes had been hailed with a shout of joy throughout England. The general feeling finds expression in a political song —or rather (we should say) a political pamphlet— in rhyming Latin verse written at the time. It is altogether a very remarkable document. It sets forth the political programme of the baronial party; it exposes all the ills under which the country had been groaning from treachery and misrule; it declares plainly—as plainly as any radical manifesto of the nineteenth century could do—that the king is bound to govern according to the laws, and (if he fails to do so) he must be taught respect for them by coercion. It lauds the patriotism and the good faith and the piety of De Montfort; it describes the struggle and the victory at Lewes; and from time to time it bursts out into pæans of triumph: "Blessed be the Lord God of Vengeance, who sitteth on His throne on high in the heavens; who by His own might treadeth upon the necks of the proud and putteth the mighty beneath the feet of the weak. He hath subdued two kings and heirs of kings, and made them captive as transgressors of the laws. May the power of the Almighty accomplish that which He hath begun and reinstate the realm of the English nation, that glory may be to Him and peace to His elect." Would you not imagine that you were listening to the utterances of some old Covenanter?

De Montfort's triumph at Lewes had been welcomed with a shout of joy. His defeat at Evesham was received with a wail of despair. It seemed as though a death-blow had been dealt to the national cause. The very heavens, so men thought, moaned and wept, and the earth shuddered over the awful catastrophe. During the battle there had been a terrible thunderstorm and earthquake; and the darkness was so intense that the priests in the churches could not see to read the prayers. For some months during the summer a great comet was visible—"a star with a lance red and clear," as it was described by writers of the time, throwing its baleful light across the skies. It had appeared about a fortnight before the battle, and it was seen for several weeks after. To its fatal influence men fondly ascribed the calamity which had befallen.

In his lifetime Earl Simon had been respected as a warrior and a patriot; in his death he was venerated as a saint and martyr. The Pope excommunicated his adherents; but the people adored his memory. Pilgrims crowded from afar to his tomb; prayer was offered for his intercession; miracles were wrought by his relics; even the dead, it was said, were raised.

The cause of liberty, of constitutional government of England, seemed for the moment to have been buried in De Montfort's grave—seemed, but it was semblance only. The blood of a political martyr, like the blood of a religious martyr, is never shed in vain. The blood of the patriot—so we may transfer the old saying—the blood of the patriot is the seed of liberty. Of Earl Simon it might truly be said, that though dead he yet spake.

And one there was—the noblest, bravest of his opponents—on whose ears this voice from the grave did not fall in vain. Prince Edward had been from first to last the life and soul of the royalist cause. The king was a comparative cipher in the struggle. In the defeat at Lewes and in the victory at Evesham Edward had borne the principal part. His fiery, passionate, reckless, impetuous chase after the Londoners had lost the day on the bare downs of Sussex. His prompt, stealthy, well-ordered march more than retrieved the disaster on the grassy banks of the Avon. When Earl Simon saw the prince and the royalist forces descending from the opposite slopes, while his own men were hopelessly, fatally entangled in the folds of the river, he was struck with admiration at the precision of the enemy's movements. "By the arm of St. James," he exclaimed, "they come on skilfully; but they have learned this from me, not from themselves." Edward *had* learnt his generalship from De Montfort; he had also learnt something better than his generalship—his loyalty to England, and to the English people. The experience of this fierce, disastrous, triumphant contest with a noble adversary had not been thrown away on the chivalrous and energetic prince. The effects were not immediately visible, but they appeared at length. This was not the first nor the last time when the mantle of the martyr—whether of religion, or of politics, or of science, of conscience and of truth in any form—has fallen on the young man who "consented unto his death."

Edward was twenty-six years old when he gained

the battle of Evesham. He was far from popular in England at this time, for he had espoused the unpopular cause. But this he had done more from the force of circumstances than from deliberate choice. His education, his sympathies, his duty, all seemed to point this way. The history of English royalty, both before and after Edward's time, furnishes too many instances of the heir-apparent to the crown leagued with the opposite faction against the reigning sovereign. If Edward had only consulted his own ambition, here was a splendid opportunity. But he was a faithful, affectionate, chivalrously devoted son. Edward did protest on more than one occasion when his father had broken his pledge; but when the bad faith of the barons in repudiating the award of St. Louis redressed the scale of justice, when he saw his father's cause in imminent danger, then, and not till then, he threw himself heart and soul into it, and he saved it.

Edward was no common person to look at. "King of men" was stamped unmistakably on his face and mien. His descendants for several generations were remarkable for their personal appearance. Even his weak, extravagant, self-indulgent son and successor was a strikingly handsome man, or rather "man-case," as Fuller quaintly puts it. Edward the First was very tall, lithe, broad-chested, and well made—"erect as a palm," says an old chronicler; "like Saul of old, from his shoulders and upwards higher than any of his people," writes another. His length of arm gave him a great advantage in wielding the spear; his length of leg secured him a firm seat on horseback. In childhood he had flaxen hair; in youth it assumed a golden hue; with manhood it grew darker; and in old age his flowing locks were silvery white. He had a broad, ample brow, and regular features. One blemish he had—his left eyelid drooped somewhat, a defect which he inherited from his father. He had, moreover, a slight impediment in his speech; but when he became animated, it would disappear, and he would pour forth a torrent of persuasive eloquence.

Of his affectionate disposition many traits are recorded. His sorrow at the news of his father's death was so poignant as to excite the astonishment, and call forth the remonstrances, of the bystanders. His respect for his mother, who had been insulted by the Londoners, instigated that fatal, furious charge along the Sussex Downs which lost the battle of Lewes. His affectionate grief for his beloved wife Eleanor, the companion of his youth and the partner of all his dangers, found expression in those splendid memorial crosses, ten in number, which in a long line, reaching from Lincoln to Westminster, marked the halting-stations of her corpse on the way to its final resting-place. The last of these, erected at a little village of Charing, within half a mile of the Abbey, has long been destroyed. But in more senses than one the days of English history are bound each to each by natural piety.

The same age has seen the re-erection of the Eleanor Cross at Charing and the building of the Albert Memorial at Kensington—the two most touching mementoes of the wedded love and the widowed sorrow of our English sovereigns.

And yet, notwithstanding all this tenderness and affection in his private relations, Edward could be perfectly terrible at times. He had inherited a dash of that furious temper which was characteristic of his race—which in its paroxysms would change his great-grandfather, Henry II., into a very wild beast, and which raged like a demon incarnate in his grandfather John. With Edward it was under control; but still it would have its occasional outbursts. On one occasion a certain Dean of St. Paul's, sent to remonstrate with the king on the heavy taxation of the clergy, dropped down dead with fear when ushered into the royal presence. On another, when his worthless son solicited an earldom for his worthless favourite, Piers Gaveston, the king seized the prince by the hair, tore out handfuls of it, and thrust him from the chamber.

And yet he was as prompt to forgive as he was quick to wrath. "Pardon him!" he once said, when his forgiveness was sought, "why, I will do that for a dog if he seeks my grace." Though resolute, even relentless, in war, he was lenient to the vanquished. After the barons' rebellion was crushed, not a single man suffered on the scaffold, though his enemies were entirely in his power.

But the characteristic feature in Edward I., even more than his courage and his magnanimity, was his integrity. He was stern, imperious, despotic, reluctant to concede anything; but when a concession was once extorted from him he loyally accepted it, however galling it might be to his proud spirit. The legend on his tomb at Westminster—*Pactum serva*, "Keep thy promise"—was inscribed some centuries after his death, nor (so far as I am aware) was the motto ever used by himself; but it well describes the man.

He was just such a ruler as our great living poet represents one of his heroes in his morbid discontent as seeking and despairing to find in our degenerate age—

> " A man with heart, head, hand,
> Like some of the simple great ones gone
> For ever and ever by,
> One still strong man in a blatant land,
> Whatever they call him, what care I,
> Aristocrat, democrat, autocrat—one
> Who can rule and dare not lie."

He was strong, and he was true.

It is no surprise to find that such a man, while he was feared by his subjects, was intensely loved and admired by them. He appeared to them to be under the special protection of heaven, and indeed his repeated hairbreadth escapes seemed to give countenance to the idea that he bore a charmed life. His wars were very costly to the people of England. The taxation was heavy. They grumbled, but they grumbled and gave. They knew that not a superfluous penny was spent on the king's personal luxuries. He was severely simple in his private habits. They knew also that when he fought (which was much too often), he fought for the glory and well-being of England, or what seemed to him to be such. They saw too—and nothing goes more directly home to a people's heart than this—that he never imposed hardships on others which he was not prepared to share himself. In the worst privations of the camp, in the severest manual labours of the siege, he insisted on bearing his part with the meanest soldier in his army.

We saw how the framework of our parliamentary constitution was completed by Simon de Montfort. But it was still only a framework. The representation of the towns was very inadequate; the purpose of the meeting was a temporary emergency; the functions of the assembled body were vague and indefinite; above all, they did not meddle with taxation.

The moment the representatives of the people got hold of the purse-strings, then their real power began. The credit of this concession belongs to Edward. He yielded it very reluctantly; he could hardly be expected to do otherwise. "He would not," says Professor Stubbs, "have been nearly so great a king if he had not thought this right worth a struggle; nor if, when that struggle was going against him, he had not seen that it was time to yield; nor if, when he had yielded, he had not determined honestly to abide by his concession." This is the gist of the whole matter. Edward's necessity was the nation's opportunity. He was constantly at war—at war with Wales, at war with France, at war with Scotland. The sinews must be provided, and these sinews must be tough and strong to bear the long continuous strain upon them. The power of the English House of Commons rose out of Edward's financial difficulties. But without Edward's loyalty the opportunity must have been thrown away.

The year 1295 may be taken as the era at which our present constitution was defined. At this crisis the king's financial difficulties were extreme. A parliament was summoned to meet at Westminster. The representation was thoroughly adequate. The sole object for which it was summoned was the *taxation* of the kingdom. The representatives of the cities and boroughs sat apart. The frankness of the king found a frank response. In the king's writ for collecting the tax it is stated, " Seeing that . . . the citizens, burgesses, and other good men of our dominions, cities, and boroughs of this same realm (of England) have granted to us courteously and spontaneously a seventh of all their movable goods, we have appointed," and so forth.

In his foreign relations, again, the policy of Edward may be regarded as an extension of the principles of Simon de Montfort. In other words, it was a distinctly English, as contrasted with a Continental, policy. His predecessors had given the first place to their Continental domains. His successors were always hankering after Continental acquisitions. The wars of Edward III. bore as their fruit some splendid hollow victories ; in their results they were useless, and much worse than useless, to England. Edward I. alone had the sagacity to discern—what we have proved by long experience—that the strength of the kingdom must lie within the four seas. For the good government and well-being of the people it must become—what happily it long has been—an island fortress. But from this point of view its territorial limits were most unsatisfactory. Wales and Scotland were still independent kingdoms. In the polite phrase, which our own age has invented as a varnish to rapine and aggression, the frontiers needed much rectification, and he was not slow to seize any opportunity of rectifying them. About his Continental provinces he showed himself singularly indifferent, while he strained every nerve to render his dominions conterminous with the four seas.

This conception, and this only, well explains his policy with regard to Wales first, and Scotland afterwards. His *motives* are capable of different explanations. But, however suspicious some of his acts may be, it is only fair to judge him by his general character. Now he was singularly free from mere selfish personal ambition. He was imperious, passionate, resolute even to obstinacy; but there was in him no taint of vainglory. In this respect he contrasts favourably with the other great warriors of his race—Richard I. and Edward III. Moreover, in his dealings with his own subjects, who ought to have known him, he had a reputation for the strictest integrity; and it would be strange if this noble quality had suddenly and wholly deserted him in his relations to others. *Nemo repente fuit turpissimus*.

Edward had too little sympathy with the feelings and sentiments of men. He treated solely as a lawyer's question what ought not to have been a lawyer's question at all. This was his great error. The age was an age of lawyers. His race—the Angevin princes—was a race of lawyers. Impressed with the enormous benefits which would flow from a union under the same crown, he eagerly seized every legal advantage which offered itself. And, unfortunately for Scotland, the chief claimants to the Scottish crown, being English barons also, yielded point after point until his case seemed to himself, whatever it might seem to others, quite complete. But meanwhile the Scottish *people* had not been consulted. A hardy and independent race, they were not reconciled to the deed of transfer by the fine parchment and the faultless engrossing.

Edward's Scottish policy paid the penalty of *precocity*. His conception was far-sighted and true, but it was premature. Time at length stepped in as a reconciler between the two kingdoms, and said,

"Sirs, ye are brothers." But three centuries were still to elapse after Edward placed the stone of Scone in Westminster Abbey before it fulfilled its prophetic destiny, and a Scottish prince, crowned thereupon, assumed the sway of Edward's dominions.

Edward had subjugated Scotland; but Scotland would not be subjugated. Again she rose in arms against her English conqueror. Edward was now sixty-eight years old. The tide of his energetic life was fast ebbing. Anxiety and toil had worn him out, for he had never spared himself. But, weak in frame, he was strong as ever in the strength of an indomitable will. He assembled his army at Carlisle and himself took the command. But the hand of death was upon him. He insisted on going forward, though he was carried in a litter and could only advance by short stages of two miles a day. For five weary days he was dragged forward. Then he succumbed. There was a strange and tragical irony in the circumstances of his death. On the shores of the Solway, with the hills of Scotland full in view, he sank exhausted into the hands of his attendants and expired. His dying injunction was, that his bones should be carried about with the army till the Scottish rebellion was quelled.

The injunction was disobeyed. He was buried peacefully in the Abbey of Westminster, then fresh from the masons' hands—there where he himself had been crowned—there where with all the mournful honours of a devoted attachment he had laid his beloved wife Eleanor—there beneath the ancient crown of Wales, the symbol of one kingdom which he had won and kept, and beside the immemorial stone of Scotland, the symbol of another kingdom which he had won and lost. His fate had been strange in life, and it was yet more strange in death. For nearly a century his tomb was opened every two years, and the cerecloth which wrapped him about was smeared fresh with wax. It would seem as though the body of the stern old king were kept ready, that some day it might be borne triumphant before the English host and take possession of the vanquished northern kingdom. But Edward's hour of vengeance never came. A change of dynasty brought peace to his remains; and he was suffered to lie undisturbed until about a hundred years ago, when he was once more exhumed to satisfy an antiquarian curiosity, and his tall gaunt form was seen for the last time.

England is strangely capricious in awarding her honours to the deceased. Imagine a foreigner, well read in English history, visiting the Old Palace Yard at Westminster for the first time, and approaching the equestrian statue which dominates the open space. Could he doubt for a moment to whom Englishmen would devote this most historic, most honourable of all sites in England? It must surely be Edward the First—Edward of Westminster— here in the place of his birth, in the place of his highest achievements—here beneath the walls of the venerable Abbey, in whose consecration and adornment he bore so prominent a part—here under the very shadow of the Parliament Houses, the shrine of the legislature which he matured, and of the Old Hall of Westminster, the seat of the judicature which he had created. The place is made for the man, and the man for the place. But no! To his astonishment he finds that the king whom Englishmen delight to honour above all kings is not the First Edward but the First Richard—a man of sinewy arm and bull-dog courage, who cared nothing for laws or judicature or constitution, or any of these things—a hero of romance, a ruffian in real life, a bad son, a bad husband, a bad man, a worse king, who bestowed upon England nothing but a contemptuous neglect and a heavy debt. Another eccentricity our foreigner will remark as he turns away—another eccentricity of these eccentric Englishmen, who are always doing such bizarre, unaccountable things!

Passing from the Palace Yard within the Abbey walls, you place yourself among the royal tombs, and another fact strikes you. While the shrine of Edward's namesake, the Confessor, rises high overhead, the centre of the group, magnificent still, though mutilated and robbed of its ornaments; while the effigy of his father rests on a lofty sepulchre rich with marbles and mosaics; while the tombs of his wife Eleanor and of his descendants Edward III. and Richard II. are surmounted by recumbent figures of gilded bronze and surmounted with decorations of elaborate workmanship; while the chantry forming a canopy over the bones of Henry V. towers aloft, a gem of architectural richness; while all around is costly and magnificent, the burial-place of Edward I. —the greatest of them all—is marked by a square stone tomb, perfectly plain, without effigy, without ornament, without even an inscription save a brief motto, a single line painted on it at a later age. But Edward's memory needs not the adventitious support of a gorgeous sepulchre. He lives in our free and progressive constitution, which recognizes the rights of all; lives in our fair and equal laws, which protect the life and property of all; lives and breathes still in all those institutions and sentiments which have made our land the "isle-altar" of Freedom.

II

IF, as an eminent historian has maintained, "the surest test of the civilization of a people—at least as sure as any—afforded by mechanical art is to be found in their architecture"; if "it is great monuments of architectural taste and magnificence that are stamped in a peculiar manner by the genius of a nation," then the civilization and the genius of England in the thirteenth century will not stand in need of any lengthy apology. If we are a little disconcerted when we reflect that our ancestors in that great age used fingers instead of forks, and closed their windows with shutters instead of glass, and fed their retainers on whale's flesh, we may go for consolation to the cathedrals and the castles, and our confidence will be restored. At all events, it seemed to me that in this second lecture, in which I purpose speaking of the intellectual as distinguished from the social and political progress of the age, I ought to give the first place to its architecture, as a monument, at once decisive and unique, of its culture and genius.

I had the hardihood on Tuesday last to throw

out a doubt whether this century had any rival throughout the whole history of architecture. I am quite aware that in saying this I am venturing on dangerous ground which will be hotly contested. I do not forget that a directly opposite opinion is sanctioned by names entitled to the highest respect: that the refined Evelyn denounces "a certain fantastical and licentious manner of building, which we have since called modern or Gothick," and denounces those "dull, heavy, monkish piles, without any just proportion, use, or beauty"; that the great architectural genius, Sir Christopher Wren, when consulted on the restoration of St. Paul's after the fire, expressed his wish to replace "the Gothick rudeness of the old design" by a new erection "after a good Roman manner"; that the accomplished Addison disparages what he calls "the meanness of manner," and the pointed style. And indeed it might be urged that such a consensus of adverse opinions, representing (as was doubtless the case) the universal verdict of their age, is in itself fatal to any exceptional claims on behalf of Gothic architecture. But I am not dismayed by this array of authorities. I am reminded that even the fame of Shakespeare underwent a similar eclipse for several generations; and my courage is quite restored by the recollection.

Indeed the time is past when men with any pretensions to taste would think of pouring contempt on the national architecture of England; and the only question worth discussing is its *relative* merit as compared with other styles. I need not stop to remark what a narrowing and depressing effect this inability to appreciate the genius of the past had, as it always will have, on the intellectual culture of the ages suffering from it. Nor will it be necessary to investigate the causes which have led to a more genial and sympathetic spirit. To your own Scott, more than to any one man, we owe it that this demon of contempt has been exorcised from the popular mind. It was impossible for a generation which had lingered entranced over the fascinations of Melrose any longer to speak, as Evelyn speaks, of those "dull, heavy, monkish piles, without any just proportion, use, or beauty." Only compare those two passages, and the contrast will serve as a measure of the change which has taken place within two or three generations.

The first passage is from the *Parentalia*, where the younger Wren gives expression to his grandfather's views on Gothic architecture.

They "soon began," he says, "to debauch this useful and noble art. . . . They set up those slender and misshapen pillars, or rather bundles of staves and incongruous props, to support incumbent weights and ponderous arched roofs without entablature; and though not without industry, nor altogether naked of gaudy sculpture, 'tis such as gluts the eye rather than gratifies or pleases it with any reasonable satisfaction."

OF THE THIRTEENTH CENTURY 143

For the second passage I need not give the reference. You will observe that the very same objects are singled out and almost the same images used to describe them :—

"The darken'd roof rose high aloof
  On pillars lofty and light and small :
The corbels were carved grotesque and grim ;
And the pillars, with cluster'd shafts so trim,
With base and with capital flourish'd around,
Seem'd bundles of lances which garlands had bound."

And again :

"Slender shafts of shapely stone,
  By foliaged tracery combined ;
Thou would'st have thought some fairy's hand
'Twixt poplars straight the osier wand,
  In many a freakish knot, had twined ;
Then framed a spell, when the work was done,
And changed the willow-wreaths to stone."

Had Scott seen the passage in the *Parentalia?* or were these coincidences and contrasts purely accidental? What will not the alteration of a word or two effect? The "bundles of staves" become "bundles of lances." The "misshapen pillars" and "incongruous props" are transmuted into "slender shafts of shapely stone." "Trim" is substituted for "gaudy," and the metamorphosis is complete. We cannot believe our eyes. The despised, slatternly, household drudge is transformed all at once into a beautiful princess.

Two styles stand out prominently in the history of architecture, the Grecian and the Gothic. The one attained its most perfect ideal in the so-called Doric of the age of Pericles; the other in the Pointed English of the age of Edward I. These two epochs will furnish the best and most characteristic examples of either style. The Parthenon at Athens and the Abbey at Westminster at once occur as typical illustrations; and no other style deserves, I think, to be placed into competition with these. I trust I am not insensible to the grandeur of individual buildings in other styles. Living, as I do, for several months in the year, under the shadow of Wren's great masterpiece, I should be guilty of unpardonable bigotry if I did not allow my sympathies to expand beyond these limits. When I contemplate the magnificent sweep of the dome rising above the picture of nave and transept, I am lost in admiration of the creative genius which produced a building where every line, curved, vertical, horizontal, is exactly in its place; and I am thankful to the fire which sacrificed one Gothic cathedral—though the largest and almost the noblest in England—to make room for such a structure. But, whatever may be the merits of isolated examples, I cannot think that any third style need be considered by the side of these two.

And the two are so utterly unlike each other, that perhaps any comparison between them may seem futile. Yet, if a preference must be declared for the one or the other, I should not hesitate to give my suffrage to the Gothic.

Coleridge, in his *Table Talk*, defines the principle of Gothic architecture as "infinity made imaginable." "It is no doubt," he adds, "a sublimer effort of genius than the Greek style." In those three words, "infinity made imaginable," he seems to me to have hit off exactly the transcendent claims of this style over its rival. Such language would be wholly out of place as applied to a Grecian temple. You might praise its stateliness, its repose, its serene beauty; but there is no suggestion of infinity in it. You feel that you have soon got to the end of it. You are conscious that you have exhausted its lessons. Greek architecture is essentially *finite*. Its forms are few and simple. When you have seen one Doric temple, you have seen all. There may be slight differences in the proportions or the dispositions of the columns; one may be more pleasing than another, but you get no new *idea*. If there is any great divergence, you set down the building as a bad example of the style. On the other hand, the combinations of Gothic architecture are simply inexhaustible. No one building is a mere counterpart of another. In the same building no one part need be like another, and yet there will be no want of harmony. What you actually see fills you with amazement, and yet you feel all the while that there are still boundless possibilities in the style lying beyond the range of actual fulfilment. This remark, of course, refers to the time when Gothic architecture was a living style. We may imitate with more or less success in these days, but it is not the same thing.

And, again, the leading conception of Gothic architecture seems to me to place it higher—I mean its *verticality*, as contrasted with the horizontal lines of the Greek. I am not now speaking of the religious ideas connected with the two styles; though I think all would acquiesce in the sentiments expressed in an eloquent passage of Dr. Charles's work, where he characterizes the Gothic cathedral as "bearing the impress of its Christian birth; whose silent finger points to heaven"; the Greek temple "as spreading along and beautifying the earth which its worshippers deified." But, as a mere question of imagination and art, is there not something far nobler in a fabric where every part, arch and buttress and pinnacle and spire, seems to breathe with lofty aspirations, than in the monotony of a repose, however beautiful, which ends in itself and leaves the eye satisfied, only because it excites no cravings? Compare the sky-line of the Parthenon with that of Canterbury or of Lichfield, and you will see what I mean.

In short, I venture to think that those who prefer Greek architecture to Gothic, ought (if they were logically consistent) to set Sophocles before Shakespeare; while those who give the palm in architecture to Palladio and to any form of Renaissance, should by analogy give it in dramatic poetry to Corneille or Racine, rather than to our own great dramatists.

An ingenious French novelist, whom I shall have to quote presently, calls Shakespeare "the last Gothic Cathedral." I accept the analogy. There are those who would prefer the *Antigone* or the *Œdipus Coloneus* to *Hamlet* or *King Lear*. I can understand the preference, but I cannot acquiesce in it. There are, or at least there were, those to whom the unities are a chief recommendation of the Greek drama. For myself I confess that rigid rules, whether in poetry or in architecture, have no great charm. They may be useful as crutches for the feeble, or as fetters for the madman, but on true genius they are a mere clog. Yet strict rules are of the very essence of Greek architecture as of Greek tragedy. In our noblest Gothic cathedrals I seem to see just the same contempt of convention, and the same confidence in genius, which I find in the greatest plays of Shakespeare.

I need not stop to inquire what was the origin of the pointed arch, the essential characteristic of Gothic architecture. It may have been a structural necessity forced upon some builder, in the first instance, by the intersection of cylindrical vaulting, and then recommending itself by its utility. It may have been an accidental idea suggested by the interlacing of semicircular arches, and, once seen, attracting the eye by its beauty. It may, like so many innovations of the twelfth and thirteenth centuries, have been a foreign importation into Europe, a legacy of the Crusades. For this view there is much to be said. But, even if this be granted, the concession detracts nothing from the glory of Gothic architecture. The true genius is he who knows how to *use* the accidental suggestion. The Saracens had done nothing to develop the power of the pointed arch, though they had been acquainted with it for centuries. With them it was rather an encumbrance than an aid to the structure. It remained simply an adventitious ornament, and not always a very graceful ornament. It had never felt the magic touch of *genius*, till it fell into the hands of European architects. Then, all at once, its magnificent capabilities were discovered. It became the very life and soul of the newly-created style. The principle of verticality, the distinctive characteristic of Gothic architecture, was wholly inspired by it; and it entered upon a career of rapid, vigorous, infinitely-varied development, which has had no parallel in the history of architecture before or after.

If we inquire after the causes of this astonishing vigour and fertility we shall find them to be twofold. It had its roots in profound religious conviction and feeling; and it enjoyed a monopoly in the domain of the imagination.

Of the profound influence which religion had in animating and fertilizing architectural genius at this time I need say little. The author of the *Enigmas of Life* imagines some ardent Protestant, whose culture is equal to his zeal, gazing in admiration at one of the great continental cathedrals, "reared in the dark days of Catholic supremacy" from "intense devotion to what he deems little less than antichristian faith," and exclaiming, despite himself, "Thank God for a false religion!" If the idea which seems to underlie this passage had been true, then indeed it were a voice *de profundis* from the very lowest depths of hopelessness and despair. But is Mr. Greg's enigma so very insoluble after all ? I have certainly no wish to excuse the corruptions and the shortcomings of the Christianity of the thirteenth century. But, on the other hand, I am old-fashioned enough to believe still that grapes are not to be gathered of thorns, nor figs of thistles. May it not be that even the worst types of religion—even the lower forms of paganism—are better than no religion at all ? better, because more real, because more true, for they recognize an actual human want which they supply, most inadequately indeed, but which the other wholly ignores. And can we regard the Christianity of the thirteenth century, despite its aberrations—the century which produced a Francis of Assisi and a St. Louis of France, which in our country saw a St. Hugh of Lincoln, and a St. Edmund of Canterbury, and a Grosseteste—as utterly base and rotten to the core ? Nay, I would ascribe these magnificent architectural results not to what was false, but to what was true in it. I see in all this nobility of design, and all this grace of execution, the fruits not of the error and the superstition, however much of both there may have been, but of the love, the devotion, the sacrifice, the public spirit of the age, the escape from self, in wider aim and loftier aspirations, which would contrast very favourably with an age in which the highest aim of men is to get on in life, and for which even its own self-chosen maxim, that honesty is the best policy, is all too arduous to act upon.

But, besides the influence of religion as the inspiring motive, I mentioned another cause which assisted largely in bringing out this marvellous result—the monopoly established by architecture in one province of the human mind. This age, as we shall see presently, was very far from devoid of literary aspirations. It was characterized by extraordinary educational activity. Its metaphysical acuteness and logical subtlety could bear comparison with those of any time, ancient or modern. Its chronicles, though not exhibiting the highest type of history, are not to be despised. But, as a vehicle of the imagination, literature had not yet got a footing in England. Indeed, from the nature of the case, this was hardly possible. Imaginative literature requires a language full, flexible, at once popular and refined. But the alternative offered at this time was inadequate for the purpose. The old literary language, Latin, was fast deteriorating—the Latin of the thirteenth century is confessedly inferior to that of the eleventh and twelfth. The literary language of the future, the native English, was still rude and unformed ; it had not yet been taken up by the cultivated classes. It is said, I know not with what truth, that there is no evidence that any one of our three first Edwards could speak a word of English. A whole century was needed after England was recovered for the English, before the language was so far developed, that the master genius of Chaucer could mould it to the higher purposes of poetry. Nor, again, had the chisel to fear a rival in the palette. We begin to hear of pictures, it is true, in the reign of Henry III., who was a great patron of all branches of art. But painting at this time was simply a *decorative* art; it had not yet entered the service of the imagination. Thus in England architecture maintained an unchallenged monopoly in this domain of human genius. My remarks do not apply so much to the South of Europe, as to the North, and more especially to England. The South had already its Provençal minstrels; and in Italy literature was soon to start forth full-grown and full-armed from the head of Zeus in the person of Dante. But in Italy and the South, Gothic architecture was always more or less of an exotic. In England and in the North of France was its true home, and its healthiest growth. Thus genius and imagination found its readiest conductor, not in the tip of the pen, but in the edge of the chisel.

In a remarkably brilliant episode of *Notre Dame de Paris*, the author discusses at length the effect of printing on the destinies of architecture. He represents a priest of the great Parisian Church pointing with his right hand to one of the earliest volumes issued from the Nuremberg press, and with his left to the huge cathedral, standing out, dark and sphinx-like, against the starlit sky, and exclaiming, "This will be the death of that. The book will kill the building." Since Guttenberg's invention, argues the author, the career of architecture has been one lingering death agony. What we call the Renaissance was, in fact, the decadence. I am not disposed to take this very gloomy view of the future of this art. But still it must be confessed that architecture has had a much harder struggle for existence since this invention gave wings to literature. A time was, when the temple or the cathedral was the most effective form in which creative genius could appeal to the public. The stone book was the most easily deciphered, the most widely read, the most importunate and self-asserting form of poetry. In the England of the thirteenth century it was, as we saw, not only without an equal, but without an antagonist. Hence imagination wrote down all her poetic thoughts in masonry—grave and gay alike—her lightest effusions as well as her most serious communings; for what else are the grotesque carvings which sometimes appear in such strange company with the most solemn subjects, but the mopings and mournings of the age, the cynicisms, the satires, possibly even the scepticism, of the mediæval mind, the imagination seeking relief in some freak of merriment or some grin of sarcasm?

But whatever may have been the causes, the

results were perfectly wonderful. It is quite clear that the architectural spirit was *in the air*. It was not concentrated in a great genius here and there, it was simply everywhere. For the most part the great stone poems of these centuries are anonymous. Here and there a name stands out from the rest, like the two Williams at Canterbury or Edward of Westminster, or Alan Walsingham at Ely; but these are only the more conspicuous figures in a race of giants, overtopping them by an inch or two and nothing more. Hence the lavish profusion of architectural works constructed during these ages. The extant buildings—wonderful as they are—can only be a small fraction of the whole number of edifices which once covered the land. Think how many have decayed by time, think how many were perhaps necessarily, but still ruthlessly, destroyed at the Reformation, and you can form some idea of the fertility of ecclesiastical architecture in these ages. It seemed, said one, as if the world had shaken itself, and throwing off the slough of age, had clothed itself with a white robe of churches. And the ecclesiastical buildings were only a portion, though quite the most considerable portion, of the whole. Edward's reign was the great epoch of castellated architecture, as the marvellous ruins of Carnarvon show. Only weigh in the one scale the extant buildings of the last fifty years of the thirteenth century, and in the other all the architectural achievements—I do not mean the masses of brick and mortar or the layers of stone, but the architectural achievement of the last four centuries and a half—and see which scale kicks the balance.

And hence, too, the rapid development of architecture during these ages. This is a fact even more remarkable than its fertility; and it contrasts strongly with the stationary character of Greek architecture. Take two Doric temples, separated by an interval of many generations, and the chief difference will be that the later work is more clumsy in its proportions than the earlier. But the architecture of the thirteenth century was growing, developing, almost from year to year, certainly from decade to decade, like a tree which is ever throwing out fresh branches, ever changing its form, always beautiful, but always new. Take the period with which I have been more immediately concerned—the period comprised in the lifetime of Edward I.—and what a succession of architectural marvels you get! The cathedral at Salisbury was among the earliest works of the period, the choir work of Henry d'Estria at Canterbury among the latest. And spanning the interval you have Exeter and Wells and Ely and Peterborough, and Lincoln and Westminster, and York and Lichfield and St. Albans and Norwich and Hereford—in several cases the greater part, in others some of the most remarkable of the building features. I say nothing of the parallel development in North France. It is only necessary to recall the names of Rheims and Amiens and Beauvais and

Chartres and Notre Dame and the St. Chapelle to stamp this period as absolutely unapproachable there, as in England, for the magnificence of its architectural masterpieces.

I would gladly dwell longer on this point, but it is time to pass on from art to literature. And first of all let me speak of the educational machinery which England owes to the thirteenth century. I must not, of course, throw any doubt on the hoar antiquity of the two great English Universities. Does not that prince among antiquarians, Anthony Wood, gravely entertain the question whether Brute, the Trojan, did not bring with him certain Greeks, and settle at Oxford more than eleven hundred years before Christ? And will not every Oxonian loyally maintain that University College was founded by King Alfred, the restorer of his Alma Mater, after a temporary decline? And, again, as regards my own University, though we cannot go so far back as Brute (of course we are sceptical about Brute), does not the school of Pythagoras stand to this hour, plain for all folk to see, testifying as stoutly as stone can testify, that the venerable sage taught the principles of Greek philosophy to a ring of naked and painted Britons in Cambridge ages before King Alfred was born? And did we not (till the other day) solemnly commemorate twice every year that renowned sovereign Egbert, king of the East Angles, and that high and mighty prince Offa, king of Mercia, among the earlier, I will not say the earliest, benefactors to our University? Why, every one knows that the image of the great goddess Diana fell down from Jupiter! Yet the sceptic will say, and for the sake of argument I will humour him, that though there are some evidences of schools at Oxford and Cambridge in the eleventh and twelfth centuries, more especially at the former, it is in the thirteenth century that the two Universities first stand out in any prominence. The earliest extant royal charters connected with either body date from the reign of Henry III.

And yet—marvellous to relate—no sooner had they started into being, than they appear in the full vigour of maturity. This is especially the case with Oxford. The day of Cambridge arrived three centuries later, when, at the epoch of the Reformation, she numbered among her sons all the great men, with hardly an exception, who piloted England through that great crisis of intellectual and religious change. But Oxford was never a greater power in England and in Europe than during the lifetime of Edward I.—Oxford, of which, as a school of learning, we hear absolutely nothing in the previous century, except an incidental notice here and there of lectures in theology or in the Pandects.

It seems probable that both Universities grew up under the shade of monastic institutions; and it is worthy of remark—I throw it out as a hint to any ladies of my audience who may be pressing the claims of their sex on academic recognition—it is worthy of remark that both owe their nurture to the patronage of ladies, Oxford to St. Frideswyde and Cambridge to St. Ethelreda.

But, however fostered, the early growth of the Universities was astonishingly rapid. Not only was Oxford, in the age of which I am speaking, more influential than she has ever been since, but her numbers were larger, very much larger, not relatively, but *absolutely*, than at any subsequent time. It is stated that there were no fewer than 30,000 students at one time within her precincts. This number, indeed, is quite incredible. However crowded the lodgings, and however meagre the fare, it is simply impossible that the Oxford of that day could have housed and fed so large a fluctuating population besides her resident inhabitants. It seems probable, as I mentioned on Tuesday, that the whole population of London at this time was not greater, or not much greater, than 30,000. But if we divide it by six and allow her 5000, as perhaps we are justified in doing, the number is still enormous. Relatively to the whole population of England, which on the most probable estimate seems to have increased tenfold, this would be equivalent to 50,000 at the present day. Of the numbers at Cambridge we have no account; but, though doubtless much fewer than those at Oxford, they must (as the incidental notices oblige us to believe) have been very considerable. From these figures, and when we reckon this among the dark ages, it will be seen that the educational activity of the country at this time was astonishing. On the other hand, it must be remembered—though the fact does not much detract from our astonishment—that Oxford and Cambridge absorbed all the education of the country, except what we should call primary education: they were grammar-schools, public schools, and Universities all in one.

A modern writer gives as the three "distinguishing traits of student life" at this time, " poverty, ardent application, and turbulence."

Of "ardent application" I can say nothing, because I know nothing. But, considering the enormous difficulties which the majority of these students must have surmounted in order to secure a university education, we may well believe that they were not indifferent to these advantages which had cost them so much. Even a generation or two ago, before the era of railways, the difficulties of getting to and from the Universities with our comparatively limited numbers were not inconsiderable. But multiply these numbers manifold, and bear in mind the want of conveyances, the scarcity of inns, the state of the roads, or rather the absence of roads, the dangers from robbers and even from wild beasts, and you will form some notion of the serious business it must have been to convey these enormous numbers to and from the University in the good old days, when Edward was king. The difficulty was met by a rough sort of organization. There were persons who did for these Oxford and Cambridge students, on a small scale, what Mr. Cook does for tourists on the Continent or in the East in our own time. They went a circuit, picked up the boys — for boys, and even little boys, many of the students were— from the several towns and villages in their neighbourhood, took them under their care, mounted them, catered for them, and provided them with lodgings, by contract, undertaking to land them in the University at the proper time. The cost was not very serious. The charge of fivepence a day, as we happen to know, covered everything, mounting as well as food and lodging, even the charge for wine being included. But, to compensate for the change in the value of money, the sum must be multiplied by fifteen or twenty before we get the equivalent in our own day. These predecessors of Mr. Cook were called "fetchers"—no bad name. Thus the students would reach Oxford at the opening of the term in cavalcades of a dozen or a score apiece, each commanded by its respective "fetchers"—a motley assemblage, boys of all ages and ranks, from the mere child of eleven or twelve to the youths of twenty or more, most of them ill-clad, ill-fed, untidy, raw, country lads, we cannot doubt, whom Alma Mater would in time lick into some sort of shape; though here and there might be found a young gentleman of quality, attended by a servant, who, like his master, purposed to avail himself of the educational advantages of the place. A strange contrast to the Oxford and Cambridge of to-day, but a contrast not in all respects favourable, I venture to think, to our vaunted nineteenth century.

And this contrast is most strongly exhibited in the general poverty of the students. We not uncommonly read of a poor student obtaining from the chancellor of his university a licence to *beg*. This issue of licences was intended to check wantoning and mendicancy; for the begging scholars were the plague of the country round. And the poverty of the student comes out in another way also. The Universities were in the habit of keeping—*horresco referens*, but I do not know how else to describe the transaction—of keeping pawn-shops at which they *accommodated* the students. And business was transacted in this way. The earliest endowments of which we read, earlier than exhibitions or scholarships, are called *chests*. In these chests, or safes, were deposited moneys, which might be lent out to needy scholars, but only on condition of their leaving as a pledge some valuable, such as an illuminated book, or a silver cup, or a hilted dagger, which was worth more than the sum borrowed, and was forfeited and sold if repayment was not made at the right time. On stated days, and with prescribed ceremonies, the chests were opened in presence of their proper guardians. New loans were issued; old loans were repaid and pledges redeemed; forfeits were appraised and sold; and the students accommodated were dismissed with an injunction to pray for the soul of the benefactor who had established the chest. The memorials of ancient poverty survived almost to our own time, and they became a scandal. The world cried shame on the practice which obtained at some colleges of servitors carrying in the dishes to the high table. It was condemned as a menial degradation. It had become an anachronism indeed; and, as an anachronism, it was best swept away. But regarded historically, it was one of the noblest relics of a noble past. It pointed to the time when the master and the servant would travel to the University together, would reside there together, would attend lectures together. But the servant did not cease to be the servant, or the master to be the master, though both were fellow-students. It was not that the student was degraded into the menial, but that the servant was elevated into the scholar. But contemptuous insolence on the one hand, and false pride on the other, spoiled all. And what nobler conception of a university than that it should welcome all, irrespective of their several stations, and should offer its advantages of learning to all, accepting social distinctions as a fact, but not letting them interfere with its own peculiar work? A university was then truly a republic of letters. The practical result of the modern spirit has been to substitute a more or less close aristocracy.

I fear that by this time I shall be set down as *laudator temporis acti*. This, however, is not at all my position. I do indeed hold that nothing is more withering in its effects, and nothing more contemptible, than a contempt for the glories of the past. But I rejoice that my lot was cast in the nineteenth century.

Another characteristic of mediæval students was their turbulence. Turbulent, indeed, they were, so fiercely turbulent that they more than once threatened the peace of the whole country. We in this nineteenth century have our town and gown rows— foolish boyish outbreaks which give much unnecessary trouble to proctors and tutors, but which never end in anything worse than a black eye, or a broken window, or (in a very extreme case) a broken bone. But the town and gown rows of the thirteenth and fourteenth centuries were perfectly awful—savage, sanguinary, devastating conflicts, which gave more trouble to the government of the day than a bread riot or a Fenian outbreak in our own age. They sometimes gave rise to serious complications between the King and the Pope; and the quarrels between the students themselves were hardly less fierce. North and South were constantly at war with each other within the precincts of the University. In order to maintain the balance and keep the peace, it was decreed that of the two proctors elected annually the one should be taken from the North, the other from the South. The same restriction was imposed on the appointment of guardians of the chests of which I have already spoken. In extreme cases these conflicts would result in wholesale migrations of students. These migrations, whatever inconveniences might have attended them, were not without their use. They gave a cosmopolitan character to academic institutions. The University of Paris—at this time the most famous in the world—served as a model to our English Universities, not only in their institutions and studies, but also in their social temperament. Early in Henry III.'s reign a general exodus of the students at Paris took place—consequent on a murderous conflict with the citizens. The University was for the time broken up. Of the students some settled in the French towns, some were invited by the English king to Oxford and Cambridge. No doubt this influx of foreign students gave a great impulse to academic education in England. But, at the same time, it set an example (if any example were needed) of turbulence on a large scale—an example which our Universities were not slow to follow. The history of Oxford at this time is a record of successive tumults—now between town and gown, now between North and South, now between nation and nation, English and Irish and Scotch, even North Welsh and South Welsh; the mayor attacking and beating and imprisoning the scholars, the chancellor fulminating excommunication against the mayor; fierce street-fights in which shops were plundered, houses burnt, and (as old Anthony Wood quaintly says), divers on both sides were "slain and pitifully wounded."

Wherever clerks gather together, said Roger Bacon, himself the Paris and Oxford clerk, whether at Paris or at Oxford, they scandalize the whole laity with their wars and disturbances and all their other vices. In fact, Oxford at this time held the same dangerous prerogative in English politics as Birmingham at the time of the Reform Bill movement, or Manchester during the Free Trade agitation. There was an old Latin rhyme which, rendered into English, runs thus :—

> "When Oxford scholars fall to fight,
> Before many months expired
> England will with war be fired."

In the year 1260 the great body of Oxford students migrated to Northampton in consequence of one of these disturbances. Turbulence is contagious. In the following year an equally fierce conflict broke out at Cambridge, with the same accompaniment of plunder and homicide. The result, too, was the same. A large number of Cambridge scholars likewise seceded to Northampton. At Northampton, this combined body of misnamed students conducted themselves with all their old turbulence and pugnacity. The war between the king and the barons was now at its height, and they took the side of the barons. When the king appeared before Northampton, "the scholars," we are told, "did with their slings, long-bows, and cross-bows, vex and gall his men more than all the forces of the barons beside; so that the king, taking notice of them, and zealously inquiring who they were, swore with a deep oath he would have them all hanged." They were not hanged, however, but ordered back to their respective Universities, and the newly-formed academic body at Northampton was broken up. In the following century there was again a wholesale exodus of the Oxford students—this time to Stamford—and again the integrity of the old University was threatened. A relic of this exodus lingered in the Oxford statute-book till comparatively recent times in the oath which was taken by every graduate, that he would "neither deliver nor attend lectures at Stamford."

But to this thirteenth century belongs not only the first contemporary recognition of the two Universities as corporate bodies, but also the rise of the collegiate system at both the two oldest colleges at Oxford. Merton and University belong to the latest years of Henry III.; the oldest foundation at Cambridge, that of Hugh de Balsham called Peterhouse, to the early years of Edward I. The rise of the collegiate system may be ascribed to the desire of providing a remedy for the two evils of academic life on which I have been dwelling—poverty and turbulence. The college in its original conception is a piece of machinery, at once for providing a maintenance for, and enforcing discipline upon, a certain number of scholars. In later times the colleges have usurped a large part of the *instruction* also; but at their first foundation this province belonged to the University. The disorderliness and the profligacy which had been found to result when so many thousand boys and young men were lodged indiscriminately in the town and subject to no supervision, led to foundations like that of Walter de Merton, whose statutes were copied by the founders of succeeding colleges. Hitherto, no doubt, the most industrious and well-behaved of the students were those who belonged to the different religious houses, such as the Franciscans and Dominicans, where they lived under control. The enlightened founder of Merton College saw what was wanted. He would have the corporate life which he found existing in the religious houses; but, as the corporate purpose of his institution, he substituted learning for religious exercises. It was especially laid down in the Merton statutes, which in the main were copied by other early colleges, that any member of the foundation who entered a religious brotherhood should, by so doing, *vacate* his fellowship or scholarship. Thus, when our colleges are spoken of as *monastic* institutions, an idea the very reverse of the truth is conveyed. A college was a distinctly *anti-monastic* institution, borrowing from the monastic bodies solely the idea of a corporate life, and distinguished from them in almost every other respect.

In speaking of Oxford and Cambridge during the thirteenth century, it is impossible, however cursory our review, to pass over one great name. Robert Grosseteste, Chancellor of Oxford, and afterwards

Bishop of Lincoln, is unquestionably the greatest *academic* personage in the history of our English Universities at *any* age. I say the greatest *academic* personage; for, though the Universities have produced greater writers, greater men of science, greater statesmen, even greater ecclesiastics, yet, as the promoter of University education, and the reformer of University life, he stands out pre-eminent. To him, more than to any one man, Oxford owes her greatness, in an age when she was greater than she has ever been since. As a man of learning, he was famous in a famous age. One of his pupils, the most magnificent genius of his time, Roger Bacon, says of him that "he alone knew all the sciences." He was acquainted with Greek and Hebrew, in an age when these accomplishments were extremely rare. As a bold, upright, unflinching reformer, his name is in all the churches. As a patriot, he may be judged from the fact that he was the friend of Simon de Montfort, the champion of English liberties. Saintly in his life, he was sainted by the common consent of the English people after his death. The Pope indeed refused him canonization. What else could be expected? Grosseteste had been the *Malleus Romanorum*, the consistent opponent of papal aggression and wrong, throughout life. It seems he had a heavy hand, says Fuller, as well as a great head. But "St. Robert" he was commonly called; and the intense veneration of succeeding ages was a more sure tribute to his virtues and his genius than any infallible decision of any infallible pope.

It was under the auspices of Robert Grosseteste that learning in our English Universities received a new impulse from a wholly unexpected quarter.

The two great orders of mendicant friars—the Dominicans and Franciscans—had started up from their cradle at once into full-grown and vigorous life. At the first opportunity they fastened upon the Universities. The Dominicans made themselves masters of Paris. The stronghold of the Franciscans was England. Already in the year 1224, two years before the death of their founder, St. Francis, they had established themselves at both the English Universities. At Oxford they were heartily welcomed by Grosseteste, who admired their zeal, their holiness, their poverty, their learning, which contrasted strongly with the idleness and ignorance and luxury of the older monastic. Yes—their *learning*. This was the remarkable fact of all. Their rivals—the Dominicans, the Preaching or Black Friars—had some excuse for indulging in human learning. The special object of their foundation was to put down heresy; and heresy could not be put down without arguing, and arguing was impossible without knowledge, and knowledge could only come of learning. But the Grey Friars, the Franciscans, had no pretext for any such indulgence. They were called into being to look after the bodies and souls of the simple poor—to feed the hungry, to nurse the leper. Their founder, St. Francis, had an undisguised distrust of books; good works, he maintained, were the only true knowledge. On one occasion when it was triumphantly announced to him that a great doctor at Paris had been received into the Order, he was much disconcerted. "I fear, my sons," he said, "that such doctors will be the destruction of my vineyard." The doctors did indeed father a wholly different vintage from that which he had expected.

I have certainly no respect for religious mendicancy as such; but justice is justice. And as a matter of justice, I protest against Hallam's language, who, after mentioning the monastic orders, curtly and scornfully dismisses "the swarms of worse vermin." I quote his words—"the swarms of worse vermin,"—the Mendicant Friars, who filled Europe with stupid superstition. What, nothing but stupid superstition? With far deeper knowledge and truer insight, a living writer, Prof. Stubbs, describes them as "always in extremes: sometimes before, sometimes after their age." We have already seen the Franciscans in the van of political progress; we see them now in the van of intellectual progress.

It is a remarkable fact that all those intellectual tendencies which we regard as peculiarly modern sprang up in the vineyard of Francis of Assisi. The champion of the experimental method, the father of scientific discovery, was the wonderful doctor, Roger Bacon. The initiator of the modern school of philosophy, which numbers among its adherents Hobbes and Locke and Mill, was the singular doctor William of Occam :—both Franciscan friars, both English schoolmen, both Oxford students.

Nor were these the only luminaries of the order in the thirteenth and fourteenth centuries. Among the English Franciscans are likewise the names of Alexander of Hales, the irrefragable doctor, who in his generation exercised a tyrannous influence over human thought equal to, or greater than, that of John Stuart Mill in our own day; and of Duns Scotus, the subtle doctor whose intellectual sovereignty was unchallenged till the eve of the Reformation, and of whom I shall have to say more presently; not to mention others famous and influential in their own day. The fact is, that the very calling of the Franciscans made them learned, as Mr. Brewer has pointed out, despite the wishes of their founder. They were necessarily great travellers, wandering from land to land, "seeing the cities of many men, and learning their modes of thought"; and thus intellectual activity was stimulated in them. They were also physicians in their homely way; and the study of the properties of simples was sufficient to provoke a scientific curiosity where the mind was predisposed. Thus they found themselves face to face with wisdom by no will of their own; and seeing her, they grew enamoured of her, the grave warnings of their simple founder notwithstanding.

Among the Oxford Franciscans, then, we find

ourselves confronted with the scholastic philosophy, and with Duns Scotus, its typical representative. England is the home of the schoolmen; and, of all the schoolmen, Duns is the most scholastic. That fickle jade fortune never gave a more capricious turn to her capricious wheel than when the name of Duns, the subtle doctor—Duns, whom Coleridge singles out as just the one Englishman gifted with a high metaphysical genius—took the place of the brainless, letterless fool. The depreciation of the scholastic philosophy which followed on the Reformation was even more unreasonable than the exaggerated reverence for it which prevailed during the two or three centuries preceding. A man like Duns Scotus could not have exercised this transcendent influence over the minds of many generations without being a truly great man. It is a libel on human nature to think otherwise. His fame in after ages has been damaged by the unreasoning veneration of his followers. His influence had become extravagant, tyrannous, crushing to the freedom of the human intellect, and it must be thrown off at all hazards. But it is an unmistakable testimony to his intellectual power. Who does not feel that the intellectual protests of Francis Bacon against the ascendency of Aristotle, are the noblest eulogium on Aristotle's greatness?

Duns Scotus is a perfect type of the schoolmen in their intense intellectual activity, in their astonishing industry, in their overwrought subtlety, in their comparative barrenness of direct results. Of his life next to nothing is known. Probably nothing was worth knowing. He lives in his books. He was the student, the schoolman, and nothing more. But, whatever country may claim him as her son, to Oxford belongs the honour of his education. At Oxford, at Paris, and at Cologne, his lectures were crowded with thousands of enthusiastic, eager listeners. The passion for logic and metaphysics must indeed have burnt intensely in those ages. He died at the early age of thirty-four, yet his works, not including sermons and commentaries, which are endless, fill thirteen closely-printed folio volumes, though (as Dean Milman describes them) "without an image, perhaps without a superfluous word, except the eternal logical formularies."

The faults of the schoolmen are very patent. Old Fuller has hit off the fundamental defect admirably. He compares them to persons living in populous towns, who, having very little ground to build upon, run their houses up high: "So," he adds, "the schoolmen in this age, lacking the latitude of general learning and languages, thought to enlarge their active minds by mounting up." The intellectual energy of the time was far in excess of the intellectual pabulum. It was a youthful, ravenous appetite, gnawing into itself. The scholastic philosophy is another mark of the *precocity* of the age.

It was all very well for Erasmus to pour scorn on the scholastic philosophy, for scholasticism was the intellectual tyrant of his age. But the tyrant has long been deposed; and it is ungenerous, not to say inappreciative, to vilify the memory of a rule, however iron-handed, which in European thought and language brought order out of chaos, and, by a paternal despotism, laid the solid foundations of a large and more liberal future. Not less considerable are the services which scholasticism has rendered to the intellectual progress of Europe. "We laugh at the quiddities of those writers now," says Coleridge, "but, in truth, these quiddities are just the parts of their language which we have rejected; whilst we never think of the mass which we have adopted, and have in daily use." Of Duns Scotus Hallam can say nothing better than that he introduced a most barbarous and unintelligible terminology, by which the school metaphysics were rendered ridiculous in the revival of literature; to Coleridge he was eminent among those "who made the languages of Europe what they now are" (*Table Talk*, 30th April 1830).

It is related of a wit of our day that he overheard a lady, as she passed by, calling his favourite dog an ugly little brute. "Oh, madam," he said, "I should like to know what he thinks of *us* at this moment." Yes, I should like to know what these old schoolmen think of us at this moment. I wish I could raise the ghost of Duns Scotus and ask his opinion about the studies of the nineteenth century. I have an uncomfortable misgiving that he might not think quite as highly as we do, of our learned discussions on antispasts and ischiorrhogics and epitrites. I question whether he would be altogether lost in admiration at the fertility and subtlety, which produces volume after volume of absolutely uncertain emendations on absolutely corrupt passages of Greek dramatists.

But among the Oxford schoolmen of this age was one who towers far above the rest, a man not of thirteenth century, but of all time. Roger Bacon ranks as a schoolman, because he was a man of learning in the scholastic age ; but in all essential characteristics, except his intellectual activity, he presents a trenchant contrast to the schoolmen.

Roger Bacon, it would appear, lived chiefly at Paris during his later life. There he lectured and there he wrote. But England claims him as her son and her scholar both. England made him what he was. Free and disrespectful, and even contemptuous, as are his criticisms of other famous men in his age, he speaks with the greatest reverence of his Oxford teachers, William of Shyreswood, and Edmund Rich (afterwards known as St. Edmund of Canterbury), and Adam Marsh, and (chief of all) Robert Grosseteste of whom I have already spoken.

At the instigation perhaps of Adam Marsh, perhaps of Grosseteste, Roger Bacon entered the Franciscan Order. Hence the main troubles of his life. His monastic vows proved a fatal clog on his studies.

Science and learning are not inexpensive. And here his vow of *poverty* interposed. To procure teachers in several languages in an age when such teachers had to be sought afar, to purchase materials and instruments for making experiments in chemistry, in optics, in mechanics, money was needed; and money he had not, and could not have. But genius always finds a way of escape out of difficulties. He importuned relations, friends, strangers. By this means he succeeded in scraping together not less than £2000—an enormous sum for that age— equivalent to some £30,000 of our own money. All this was spent on his scientific or literary pursuits.

But another difficulty still remained. If his vow of poverty stood in his way, his vow of obedience was a still greater hindrance. He could write nothing, could publish nothing, without the express permission of his Superior. But in that unscientific age, all scientific investigation was looked upon with suspicion. The man who, by patient research, had extorted some new secret from Nature, was thought to have sold himself to the evil one. Science was denounced as witchcraft, the natural philosopher was suspected as a magician. Under these circumstances he was not likely to find much favour with his superiors. He was thwarted at every turn.

Thus he fought against neglect, against suspicion, against disadvantages and difficulties of every kind.

"To feel himself superior in wisdom," says a living writer, "to all around, and find them preferred before him; to see his knowledge of Greek, Hebrew, Arabic slighted, whilst their miserable Latin was applauded . . . to spend many months in constructing a burning mirror and crystal spheres and astronomical tables, and to see that no one cared about them; to feel that he stood alone on the pinnacle of the highest and most mysterious science, and ought to have been honoured by kings and princes, while he was only a mendicant friar suspected and worried by his brothers—this must have been the great and bitter trial of his life."

And it is plain that a sense of neglect did rankle in his heart. He once complains that his name has been buried in oblivion for the last ten years. He quotes with bitterness the old proverb: "It is folly to give lettuces to a donkey, when thistles are good enough for him."

At length, however, the light flashed in upon his obscurity; and it flashed from the most unlikely quarter. The reigning Pope was Clement IV. England did not owe him any thanks: he set himself steadily against her national liberties; he excommunicated the adherents of de Montfort; he absolved the king from his pledges; he declared the charters null and void. But to his eternal honour be it said, that he found out Roger Bacon and drew him forth from his obscurity. As cardinal and legate he had visited England and heard of, perhaps seen, the marvellous Oxford scholar. And now that he had assumed the papal tiara, he invited Bacon to send him what he had written on science and philosophy.

Bacon had written nothing; he was not allowed to write; but he had stored his mind with a mass of learning, had gone through an amount of research which (considering the hindrance of the age) would be quite incredible, if it had not been quite indisputable.

The Pope's command overruled all the restrictions of his order. He was free to publish now; and the long-pent-up stream poured forth in a flood of knowledge and thought and research. It was at the very time when the struggle between the king and barons was being fought out to its bitter end that Clement's letter reached him. It fired him with a new enthusiasm. In less than a year and a half he completed three large works comprising original research, independent thought, extensive information on all known branches of study — languages, astronomy, geography, mathematics, optics, chemistry, ethics, theology. This was the one bright epoch in Roger Bacon's life — these eighteen months of unremitting, self-devoted, enthusiastic toil. In the whole history of literature no such marvellous feat is recorded as this effort of the poor Franciscan friar in the thirteenth century. Bacon's work has been aptly described as the *Encyclopædia* and the *Novum Organum* in one. He had well earned the title of the wonderful doctor, *Doctor Mirabilis*.

The most marvellous feature in this marvellous product is its freedom from the trammels of the age. Indeed it is so independent as to be almost reactionary. Logic was the passion of the thirteenth century. Of logicians Bacon speaks slightingly. Law, especially canon law, dominated everywhere. For jurists Bacon has only contempt. The two portals of knowledge with him are languages and mathematics, the terms being used by him in a comprehensive sense—both branches of knowledge altogether neglected by his contemporaries and for generations to come, both at length exalted to the first place in the academic studies of modern times. Indeed there is hardly any great intellectual development of later ages of which you cannot trace a germ in Roger Bacon. In the exposition of the true scientific method he is the precursor of Francis Bacon; in natural philosophy of Isaac Newton; in Biblical interpretation of Erasmus; in philology of Bentley and of Bopp.

But hardly less wonderful is the scientific foresight or the scientific enthusiasm which leads him to predict those splendid victories over nature, of which some have been realized only in this nineteenth century, and some still remain to be realized, but doubtless will be realized hereafter. Take, for instance, this which was fulfilled in the *telescope*, "We might (by means of glasses) make the sun, moon, and stars come lower down to us"; or this in the *tubular and suspension bridges*, "Bridges may be made across rivers without piers or other support"; or this in the *diving bell*, "Contrivances also may be made for walking at the bottom of the sea or rivers without danger to the body"; or this in the *steamship*, "Vessels may be borne along under the guidance of a single man with greater speed than if they had been full of sailors"; or this in the *locomotive*, "Carriages may be constructed so as to be moved without any animal power with an incalculable impetus"; or this which is not yet realized in the *aeronaut*, "Machines also for flying may be made, so that a man seated in the middle may turn round a certain mechanism by which artificial wings may beat the air, flying like a bird." Of all his wonderful predictions these "argosies of magic sail" alone await fulfilment, a vision of the future still to the laureate of the nineteenth century as they were to the philosopher of the thirteenth. "The wise," says Roger Bacon magnificently, "the wise are now ignorant of many things, which will be known to the common herd of learners in time to come."

But there is yet one other discovery which Bacon appears to have made, and of which he speaks vaguely, that must not be passed over in silence. While the armies of Simon de Montfort and Prince Edward were fighting with such weapons as the age afforded—beating out each other's brains with maces, and hacking at each other's arms and legs with battle-axes, and piercing each other with arrows— this poor student had hit on a secret which was destined to expel maces and battle-axes and bows and arrows altogether, and to revolutionize the whole character of warfare. He suggests that children's fireworks, made of saltpetre, might lead to the construction of a terrible engine of war, which should destroy armies and batter down cities.

Strange utterances these to issue from the cell of a bare-footed friar; and yet, intermingled with all this keen intelligence, all this scientific foresight, with all this large appreciation of the true bases of human knowledge, are occasional puerilities which seem to remind us that we are in the thirteenth century still. Thus he can discuss gravely how the comet which appeared about the time of the battle of Evesham was generated by the virtue of Mars, and therefore excited men to anger, discord, and wars; and relate, as an unquestionable fact, how the flying dragons in Ethiopia are caught by the inhabitants, saddled and bridled and ridden hard by them to make their flesh tender; then they are killed, and the flesh, duly prepared, is eaten as a preservative against the accidents of old age, and so he adds, in his most serious mood, "They prolong life and refine the intellect beyond all belief." Beyond all belief indeed! Roger Bacon is a true type of the thirteenth century, a great but premature intellect which has outgrown itself;

and these lectures, to which you have listened so kindly, cannot more fitly close than with a notice of this poor Franciscan friar, a magnificent and precocious genius in a magnificent and precocious age.

THE CHAPEL OF ST. PETER AND THE MANOR-HOUSE OF AUCKLAND

AN ATTEMPT TO ELUCIDATE SOME POINTS IN THEIR PAST HISTORY

ON St. Peter's Day 1665 Bishop Cosin consecrated the present chapel, and named it after the Apostle whose festival was being celebrated. The choice of the day was probably determined by the choice of the saint, rather than conversely. There were many reasons which might lead Cosin to dedicate his new chapel to St. Peter. Locally, it would be very appropriate, as the Parish Church of Auckland bears the name of St. Andrew, and this fact might suggest his brother and fellow-apostle for the new dedication. Personally, this name would have special attraction for Cosin. Both the offices which he held before the troubles, from which he had been ejected during the Commonwealth, and in which on the Restoration he had again been replaced for a short time prior to his promotion to Durham, commemorated this Apostle. He was dean of the venerable minster which gives its name to the city of Peterborough. He was master of the most ancient society in the University of Cambridge, St. Peter's College.

A large congregation of the principal laity and clergy of the diocese was assembled on the occasion of its dedication, including the dean and prebendaries of Durham. The sermon was preached by Dr. Davenport on the text, "He is worthy for whom he shall do this, for he loveth our nation, and he hath built us a synagogue," etc. The preacher "moved all the clergy and laity to be persuaded, by the sight of the beauty of this chapell, to repair and beautify their own churches and chancells."

But a glance round will suffice to show that portions of the building are at least four centuries earlier than this date. The arcades can hardly be dated later, or much later, than the middle of the thirteenth century. What, then, was the previous history of building ? How did it assume its present condition and appearance ? What did Cosin mean by his consecration of it ?

It has been generally assumed that Cosin only repaired and altered the existing chapel ; that the building had served the same purpose all along ; and that by consecrating, or rather reconsecrating, it Cosin merely intended to purge it from all the defilement which it had undergone during the Parliamentary wars and the troubles of the Commonwealth. This assumption is made by Raine, the accomplished author of the monograph on *Auckland Castle*, who, accordingly, does not trouble himself with discussing the notices which he has collected with so much learning and assiduity. The building stands east and west, as a chapel ought to stand. It has a central nave and side aisles, after the manner of an ecclesiastical building. In short, it has every appearance of having been destined to its present use from the beginning.

184 THE CHAPEL OF ST. PETER AND

Yet the notices of the ancient chapel of Auckland Castle before the Commonwealth are such as to suggest the gravest misgivings, when confronted with this assumption; and these misgivings are confirmed by the accounts of Cosin's actual work at the Restoration. I shall endeavour to piece together these data so as to construct, as far as possible, a continuous history of the chapel. While doing so, however, it is only fair to premise that I am very largely indebted for the information collected to Raine's *Auckland Castle*, so that I am using against him the weapon which he himself has placed in my hands.

1. The *origin* of the chapel in the bishop's manor-house at Auckland is veiled in obscurity. The first notice of such a building refers to the year 1271, during the episcopate of Robert de Stichell, where it is mentioned as the scene of a certain transaction between the Archdeacon and Prior of Durham, which took place there in the presence of the bishop. On the other hand, Graystanes ascribes the erection of the chapel to Anthony Beck (A.D. 1283-1310). So also Leland speaks of this magnificent prelate as building an "exceeding goodly chapelle, of stone welle squared"; and later writers, as Godwin and Dugdale, hold similar language. The attribution to Beck is confirmed by the accounts of this prelate, in which we find a payment made "to Galfrid, the bailiff of Auckland, for building the Chapel of Auckland, £148." This refers to the twenty-fifth year of his "pontificate" (*i.e.* probably A.D. 1308). In these same accounts there is likewise a charge for "wax bought for the chapel."

It is impossible to say whether Beck pulled down the

former chapel existing in Robert de Stichell's time and replaced it by another, or whether he completed a structure begun before his own time. The sum named, £148, would be worth, in purchasing value, as much perhaps as £2000 in our own day; but this would be insufficient to erect such a structure as the chapel of the manor-house seems to have been. Yet, as only one year's accounts of this prelate are preserved, there may have been other payments in preceding or succeeding years for this same purpose. Altogether it is a safe inference that the chapel was built mainly, if not wholly, by him; and there is good reason to believe that it remained substantially as he left it till the time of the Commonwealth.

2. The notices also reveal something of its *architectural character*. The next reference to the chapel after Anthony Beck's time is in the accounts (A.D. 1337-38) of Richard de Bury, where we meet with an item for the purchase of tin for "repairing the Chapel"; while just below there is an entry of a payment to the plumber for soldering "in the great Chapel and the little Chapel." Again somewhat lower down is another disbursement "for repairing the windows of the great Chapel against Christmas." Thus the chapel is spoken of sometimes in the singular, sometimes in the dual. Another notice, a century and a half later, in Bishop Booth's time (A.D. 1471-72), reveals a difference not only in size, but in level. There are two entries in his accounts, one for repairing "the great Chapel," the other for cleaning "the high Chapel" ("alta capella"). So, again, in the accounts of his immediate successor Dudley (A.D. 1476) there is an item for stopping up a window in "the high Chapel," the

same expression as before. Another notice in the same direction occurs in Tunstall's accounts (A.D. 1547-48) where mention is made of the removal of "the stalles in the hye Chapel"—a notice to which I shall have to recur at a later point. As Tunstall was the last pre-Reformation bishop, so Pilkington was the first occupant of the see after the Reformation (A.D. 1561-75). During his episcopate, again, we hear of the two chapels, though they are described in terms which would have led us astray, if we had not been able to interpret them by other information: "The lower part of the said Colledge [of Auckland] where divine service had been duly celebrated"; "The house above the said Colledge which before tyme had been used by the said churchmen for divine service." The language thus employed I will consider more fully when I come to speak of the college. I would only remark here, that these two places, in which divine service was held, cannot well be understood otherwise than as referring to the high and low chapels of other notices. This becomes the more evident, when we find that such notices are continued after Pilkington's time. Thus under Barnes, his immediate successor, several items relating to the chapel appear in this prelate's accounts, among others one for "one paire of bands for a dore in the heighe Churche." Again in Neile's inventory (A.D. 1628) mention is made of "the lowe Chapple, the lower Chappell." In a letter of this same bishop, dated 20th December 1621, he mentions a payment to one John Lockey of "£5 of his agreement with me for the east window of Auckland chappell." A few years later (A.D. 1634) Sir W. Brereton paid a visit to Bishop Moreton, of which he has left an account. As I shall have occasion to refer to them more than once, I will give his words in full:—

"Two chapels belonging hereunto (the bishop's palace at Auckland), the one over the other; the higher a most dainty, neat, light, pleasant place, but the voice is so drowned and swallowed by the echo, as few words can be understood. The lower is made use of upon Sabbath days, where, 21 Junie, Dr. Dod, now Dean of Ripon, made an excellent sermon; great resort hither on Sabbath by the neighbourhood; one sermon in morning, and prayers in the afternoon."

Then came the great catastrophe. The Parliamentary Survey (A.D. 1646), in the summary prefixed, speaks of "two Chapels to it (the manor-house of Auckland) one over the other"; and in the body of the Survey there is another mention of "the two chapels." Again the "High Chapel" is twice mentioned in this document; and the two notices throw some light on its character. In the one the dilapidations include "At the end of the High Chapel two doors," and in the other, "For the top of the High Tower above the stairs and the High Chaple wanting 576 feet of stone for embattlements." In the latter notice the reference to the "High Tower" will need explanation hereafter, but I shall dismiss it for the present. The former should be supplemented by another item in this same Survey: "For bands for three doors at the end of the Chapel." Whether "the chapel" here includes both upper and lower chapel, or designates either singly, it is impossible to say. Another entry in another part of the Survey should be mentioned, "In the landing adjoining to the Chapel 5 doors." This suggests, what would be probable enough in itself, that the upper chapel was approached from the first floor of the house, and the five doors would lead to apartments, etc., on the same landing.

The reader will have perceived at once that these notices are wholly irreconcilable with the existing chapel. The existing structure is one single and complete whole. It could not have been spoken of indifferently as a "chapel" or chapels. The construction of a chapel in two stories was not uncommon. We have examples in royal palaces, such as the Sainte Chapelle in Paris, and St. Stephen's, Westminster. But this construction seems to have been especially affected in the larger Episcopal residences. The chapel at Lambeth may serve as an example. Here, however, the lower chapel is strictly an underground crypt. Better illustrations of the structure at Auckland will be found in France. Such, for instance, are the existing Archiepiscopal chapels at Laon and at Rheims, which have an upper and a lower chapel—the structure being entirely above ground. Such was the Archiepiscopal chapel at Notre Dame de Paris till it was destroyed in the tumult of 13th February 1831. These foreign examples, indeed, terminated at the east end, after the usual French manner, in an apse, whereas Beck's structure at Auckland seems from the notice quoted above (p. 186), from a letter of Bishop Neile, to have had a large east window, as we should expect in an English building, and as the present chapel at Auckland has. But this does not affect the pertinence of the illustration for the purpose for which it is adduced. In the Laon chapel for instance, which I have visited, the upper chapel is on the level of the first floor and is approached from a doorway on the landing.

Raine, being carried away by his prepossession, overlooks all these examples, identifies the present chapel with the greater chapel of the pre-Restoration period, and looks about in vain for the lesser chapel. He describes Bishop Tunstall as removing the stalls (see above, p. 186) "from the upper or *minor* chapel," and throws out the suggestion, "It appears to have occupied that portion of the fabric now converted into bedrooms immediately above the present porch of the lower Chapel." On this hypothesis, his identification of the lesser chapel with the upper becomes a necessity; but everything points, as a close examination of the notices will have suggested already, and as we shall see more fully presently, to the high chapel as the more spacious and more magnificent and more important structure of the two, and therefore deserving the epithet of "greater." If the lost second chapel (which he regards as the lesser) must be identified with any part of the existing structure, the identification with the portion on the first floor, containing the two bedrooms which open into each other, and whose windows look down on the north terrace, is the only possible solution. But there is nothing at all in these rooms to suggest the venerable antiquity, or the ecclesiastical character, which befits the notices of the minor chapel. Nor again are they, in any strict sense, "over" or "above" the present (supposed "lower") chapel. Nor, lastly, would they explain the fact that "the chapel" is "frequently" spoken of in the singular; for they are quite a separate block of buildings, and do not even range in the same line with it.

3. After discussing the *architectural features* of the old chapel, let me say something about its position. The first notice which leads to any result appears in the

accounts of Cardinal Langley for the year A.D. 1422-23, where payments are entered as made to a carpenter for several doors, one of them a "postron on the south side of the Chapel opening into the highway." This is inconsistent with the position of the present chapel which is situated on the north side of the castle, and whose south side lies within the court, so that a highway cannot possibly have run along it. Clearly the chapel occupied the south side of the court, facing the present chapel; and the highway in question would correspond roughly to the present carriage drive, which runs along the outside of the boundary wall to the south. This position is further confirmed by the Parliamentary Survey, which speaks of "the rooms on the level of the north side to the Chapel and the south side," *i.e.* of the castle. Lastly, what is clearly enough indicated in these two notices of different dates, is directly stated by Dugdale, whose words are worth quoting at length, as I shall have to refer to it again.

"Whereas that ancient castle (one of the chief mansions of this bishop) was, upon the seizure of the bishop's lands by the late usurpers, bestowed on Sir Arthur Haselrigg of Rousby, in the county of Leicester, Bart. (a member of their then House of Commons, and in those unhappy times one of the most violent actors against the king and church). He, designing to make that place (*scil.* Aukland) his principal seat, not liking the old-fashioned building of the Castle, resolved therefore on a new structure of a most noble and beautiful fabrick, all of one pile, according to the most elegant mode of those times; taking for his pattern that curious and stately building at Thorpe near Peterborough in Northamptonshire, which Oliver St. John had after the murder of the king newly erected," etc.

THE MANOR-HOUSE OF AUCKLAND 191

" To fit himself, therefore, with materials for this his new house, he pull'd down a most magnificent and large Chappel standing on the south side of the Castle at Aukland; which Chappel was built in the time of King Edward I. (near CCCC. years since) by that great prelate Anthony Beke, then Bishop of Durham, and Patriarch of Jerusalem (of whom I have already made mention), with the stone whereof, and an addition of what was deficient, he erected the new fabrick in a large court on the east of the Castle.

" But this worthy bishop, soon after his consecration, taking notice that the greatest part of the materials made use of in that building were what were taken from that consecrated Chappel, not only refused to make use of it for his habitation, tho' it was most commodiously contrived and nobly built; but took it wholly down, and with the stone thereof built another beautiful Chappel on the north side of that great court."

After which he gives an account of Cosin's grave, and writes out at length the inscription written by Cosin for his tomb, in which he records of himself—

QVI · HOC · SACELLVM ·
CONSTRVXIT · ORNAVIT · ET · CONSECRAVIT ·
A.D. · MDCLXVI · IN · FESTO · S. PETRI.

Dugdale is quite explicit here. He states that the old chapel stood on the south side of the great court, and that Cosin's new chapel was built on the north side. But Dugdale is an unexceptionable witness. He was acquainted with Cosin. He made a heraldic visitation of the county in the year of Cosin's consecration of his new chapel, and two pen-and-ink sketches of the castle made 4th September 1666 by Gregory King, who was in attendance on him on this occasion, are extant in the College of Arms.

Thus the position resists the identification of the old chapel with Cosin's new chapel, as decidedly as the architectural character was shown to resist it.

4. *The Connexion with the College*, which commenced in the middle of the fifteenth century, is a highly interesting and important episode in the history of the old chapel ; but this subject must be left till I have occasion to speak of the college.

5. *The Dismantling and Demolition of the Chapel* covers a period of a century or thereabouts. It may be said to have commenced with the action of Tunstall, in whose accounts (A.D. 1547-48) is a payment for "takyng downe of the stalles in the hye chapell, and sortynge of them, and dyghtinge and dressinge of them, and helping to convey them to Durram." Tunstall was at this time building his new chapel in Durham Castle, and they were transferred for the purpose of furnishing it. These are the beautifully carved stall-ends which may still be seen in the Durham Chapel, bearing the arms of Ruthall (A.D. 1509-22), so that they can only have been some thirty years old when they were removed to their new home. But why did Tunstall take this step ? No doubt it was a great convenience to him to find such handsome carved work ready to hand. But he was not parsimonious ; his work elsewhere, both at Auckland and at Durham, bears testimony to his munificent and architectural constructive spirit. He was the very reverse of his successor Pilkington in this respect, and had nothing of the iconoclast or the destroyer in him. I seem to see the reason in a later

THE MANOR-HOUSE OF AUCKLAND

notice. The acoustic properties of his "High Chapel," though architecturally so beautiful, were vilely bad. Thus it was practically useless; and Tunstall had the less scruple in removing such furniture from it as was needed for his Durham Chapel.

Then came the Reformation, and Pilkington with it (A.D. 1561). His treatment of the chapel is thus described in an anonymous writer:—

"Likewise he . . . brust in peaces the college bells of Auckland, and sould and converted them unto his use; and in the lower part of the said Colledge, where divine service had been duly celebrated, he made a bowling alleye, and in the howse above the said Colledge, which before tyme had been used by the said churchmen for Divine service upon generall festivall daies, he builte here a paire of buttes, in the which two places he allowed both shooting and bowling."

The two places here mentioned can be none other than the high and low chapels, as I have said already (p. 188), and hope to show more fully hereafter. As regards the high chapel, we are thus informed that it had for some time past been partially disused. Whether "before tyme" refers to the period before or the period after Tunstall's dismantling, or includes both, we cannot say decisively. But it would seem probable that services would be held there after this event, though only at rare intervals—this having been the practice in analogous cases, so as to sustain the sacred character of the building —and that, therefore, the dismantling was only partial. On the other hand, the "Low Chapel," which had no such acoustic disabilities, was in everyday use until Pilkington's accession. Pilkington completed the partial dismantling of the high chapel, and turned it into an archery ground; while he stripped the lower chapel and made a bowling alley of it. Probably he said family prayers in the dining-room or the drawing-room. The idea of sacrilege had no place in his mind.

Pilkington's successor, Barnes (A.D. 1575-1587), has never had justice done to him. He showed himself in many respects a vigorous administrator of the diocese; he repaired many of Pilkington's injuries done to the property of the see; and he appears to have done something towards repairing the ruinous condition of the chapel. In his accounts during the earlier years of his occupation (A.D. 1577-78; A.D. 1580-81; A.D. 1581-82) there are several payments for work done in the chapel—carpentry, iron casements, window bars, "trellesses," etc. He seems to have made the upper chapel externally sound, for he pays for "one paire of bands for a dore for the heighe churche"; and, if I mistake not, he refitted the low chapel for divine service. The stall-ends, which Cosin found somewhere in the castle, and directed to be "wrought over by the carver with his tooles to appeare like new worke, artificially repaireing the mitres and what is decayed," and which still stand where they were placed by Cosin, are considered by Raine to "have been of" the date of about 1600, or perhaps a little earlier. Were they not part of the refitting of the lower chapel by Barnes, to which the notices seem to point? The "decay" would be easily explained by their lying about uncared for, perhaps in the open air, since the old chapel was finally demolished by Haselrigg.

At all events, from this time forward we find the low chapel again in use, whereas the high chapel seems to have been abandoned. Thus in Neile's inventory (A.D. 1628) we find:—

"IN THE LOWE CHAPPLE.—Item, a comunion table, foure long joyned formes of dale bords, and a litle table with a litle cupbord under it, a long firdale mast (*sic*), two long ladders of firdales, two short ladders of firdayles, and two other short ladders of oake, and a cover of a pulpitt."

But there is no mention of the high chapel, so that we must suppose it entirely bare. Again, six years later, when Sir W. Brereton visited Bishop Moreton (A.D. 1634), as we have seen (p. 187), service was held and sermons were preached on Sundays in the lower chapel, to which large numbers of persons resorted from the neighbourhood; but it is implied that no use was made of the high chapel on account of the echo which rendered the speaker inaudible.

Moreton was the last bishop who preached or performed the service in the old chapel. He was still in possession of the see when the revolutionary troubles came, and this ancient Episcopal manor-house was sold to Sir Arthur Haselrigg. How he dealt with the chapel, we have already heard in the passage of Dugdale. It was no longer in existence in 1659, when Barwick preached his funeral sermon over Moreton, for he writes:—

" To the same effect spoke Basire in his funeral sermon over Cosin, published under the title, 'Dead Man's Real Speech'" (p. 77).

" He did erect a goodly chapel in the castle of Auckland, consecrated by himself on St. Peter's Day 1665; two goodly chapels, formerly erected there (in which I have also officiated for some years of peace) being blown up by Sir Arthur Haslerig in the *Gunpowder Plot* of the late *Rebellion.*"

It would seem that Basire did not mean his expression to be taken literally. If Sir Arthur Haselrigg intended to use the materials for his own house, as he is said to have done, this mode of disintegrating the ancient work would have been a very sorry preparation. Yet a literal interpretation is put upon it by Smith, who writes (*Vita Cosini*, p. 25): "Sacellum Aucklandiæ, flagrante rebellione Parliamentaria pulvere pyrio eversum, e fundamentis extruxit." This writer is obviously ill informed. Not only does he mistake the nature of the "Gunpowder Plot," but he treats the new chapel as rebuilt on the foundations of the old. On the other hand, Barwick and Basire, both well acquainted with the place and its history, treat the new chapel as a different structure, and both speak of the two chapels prior to the Restoration, as we have heard them spoken of again and again, from the days of Richard de Bury onwards.

Thus also is the language of Cosin himself.

But, if the present chapel was not the original chapel of the bishop's manor-house of Auckland, what was it? To this question there can be only one answer. It was undoubtedly, as Mr. Longstaffe was the first to suggest, the hall of the pre-Restoration building. We should be forced to this conclusion by a process of exhaustion, if we had no other evidence. There is no other portion of the older building with which it could be identified. The great chamber is the present large drawing-room. The great dining-room has borne its present name uninterruptedly since it was built in the first half of the sixteenth century. What then remains? Raine has a solution to offer. "If any portions of that hall," he writes, "now remain, they may probably be found in the present kitchen." But he continues, "its pillars, however, are of stone, whilst those of Beck are stated to have been of marble" (p. 102). Thus he answers himself. His suggestion is the suggestion of despair. The exhaustive process therefore brings us to the present chapel. But it is more important to observe that the present chapel answers in all particulars to the hall, both in position and in character. Lastly, in the Parliamentary Survey (1646) we read in two different places of the west *end* of the hall.

1. The old hall certainly ran east and west, as the present chapel does. In other words, it was orientated. This we learn from Tunstall's accounts (A.D. 1543-44), where mention is made of the north and south *sides*, but not the west *end* of the hall. So, again, in Bishop Neile's time (A.D. 1628) we meet with "the north side of the hall."

2. We hear as early as Richard de Bury's time (A.D. 1337 - 38) of "the close under the hall," which is excepted from the rest of the summer pasture of the park in a certain sale. The same field is called lower down the "Hall Meadows" (halmedues). Again, in Hatfield's time, we find that the pasture below the hall is excepted from sale, and reserved, as it was in Richard de Bury's, and accordingly there is an item for palings round the close beneath the hall. Again in Booth's accounts (A.D. 1471-72) we come across the same name which we met with a century earlier, the "Hall Meadow" (halmedow). But this is the only position within the castle in which the hall could have stood, so as to overhang a meadow

and give its name to it. The meadow is now known as the "low pastures."

3. It is not too fanciful to see an indication of this position in another fact. In Tunstall's accounts charges occur for glazing the windows of the hall; but 18 feet of glass are required for the north side and 4 feet for the west end, whereas only 2 feet are wanted for the south side. Now the north side of a building situated here would be especially exposed to wind and storm, sweeping unchecked over the plains northward of the castle; and we learn accidentally in the accounts of the previous year (A.D. 1541-42), that "the grett barne was perysshyd in the great wind," so that there had been a violent hurricane not long before. A later notice in Sanderson's Diary (17th May 1685) shows how disastrous a storm might be to this building. "A great storm of thunder at Bishop Auckland; hailstones five inches round; the glass windows were broken; the bishop's chapel cost about £25 repairing."

4. Having discussed its position, I turn to its character and features; and I find Sir W. Brereton, whose visit to Bishop Moreton (A.D. 1634) I have mentioned already, describing it as "a very fair, neat hall, as I have found in any bishop's palace in England." Of the force of the epithets here used we may form an estimate from the fact that in the same paragraph he calls the high chapel "a most dainty, neat, light, pleasant place." Considering that Brereton must have seen Lambeth, not to mention other Episcopal residences, we may safely assume that the hall at Auckland must have been no ordinary building to bear the palm among them all.

5. But a more definite description is given by Leland

THE MANOR-HOUSE OF AUCKLAND 199

(A.D. 1532-52), who writes (*Itinerary*, i. p. 73, ed. Hearne: Oxford, 1770): "Antonius de Beke . . . made the greaut Haulle, there be divers pillors of blak marble spekelid with white." The clustered columns in the present chapel, where every alternate pillar is of Stanhope or (more properly speaking) Frosterley marble, quarried in the neighbouring Weardale, would (when they retained their polish) exactly answer to this description. The dark pillars in Durham Cathedral are of this same marble, which closely resembles the Purbeck.

6. Again, in old notices of the original hall at Auckland, during the episcopates of Dudley (A.D. 1480-81) and Tunstall (A.D. 1543-44), we find mention of a "lovir" or "lover," *i.e.* a louvre, which was a very common and indeed characteristic feature of an ancient hall, as *e.g.* at Trinity College, Cambridge. Now in Cosin's instructions, which are communicated in a letter (dated February $166\frac{1}{2}$) from Arden to Stapylton, who superintended the work, is told that "My lord means the same lanthorne that is over the Chapell shall be so, though the roof be altered, and he will have a lanthorne like it also over the new hall." The new hall mentioned here is the present great drawing-room—the room which was previously called the great chamber, but became a hall when the original hall was transformed into a chapel. The "lanthorne" was actually erected in pursuance of these directions; for at a later date (30th August 1664) Cosin gives orders for the completion of "the lanthorne" of the great hall chamber; and accordingly it appears as late as Buck's print (A.D. 1728), but has since been removed. A similar lanthorne or louvre, then, stood on the roof of the present chapel, before the clerestory was erected by Cosin,

and it had been his first intention that it should remain (or rather be replaced) notwithstanding the raising of the clerestory, but he seems afterwards to have changed his mind ; perhaps on second thoughts he saw the incongruity, and he may possibly have utilized this very "lanthorne" for the "new hall," where it would not be out of keeping.

7. The highly probable conclusion to which all these notices irresistibly tend was converted into a certainty by the results of recent discovery. Three or four years ago the plaster reredos which had been erected in the last century was removed (the plate, Raine, p. 92, represents the condition of the wall), and the east wall was thus laid bare. The remains of the arches of three doorways were revealed. The level at which persons entered through these doorways was several feet lower than the present floor of the chapel. Considerably above these arches, and not far below the plinth of the present window, were the joists of beams which supported the roof of a building running lengthwise along the east end of the chapel. In fact, it presented all the features which might be looked for in an ancient hall. The visitor, on entering, would find himself on the lower level ; stepping forward he would mount a flight of steps by which he entered into the main hall. This arrangement may be seen at the deanery in Durham, where the entrance-hall is part of the original dining-hall of the prior's residence. Evidently the three doors led to the offices which were contained wholly or in part in this building, which ran along the east end of the building as described.

I should add also that at the east end of the exterior

of the north wall there are traces of a door (at a higher level), which was apparently approached by a flight of steps, and may have led to a minstrels' gallery or to a reader's pulpit.

The significance of this discovery will be seen at once from the following passage in Willis and Clark's *Architectural History of Cambridge*, iii. p. 372 *sq.*—

"The description and plan of Haddon Hall (p. 271) shows that the passage entered from the hall-porch contained, on the side opposite to the doors of the hall, three openings. That in the centre led through a long passage to the kitchen, and the two others, in this instance, opened into the buttery and wine-cellar respectively, the pantry being placed between the cellar and the kitchen, and entered from the passage leading to the latter. In most examples it is entered directly from the through-passage at the lower end of the hall. This arrangement of three doors leading to the buttery, kitchen, and pantry respectively, which Professor Willis calls 'the triple arcade,' was the normal arrangement of a mediæval manor-house, and was copied in most of the older colleges at Cambridge."

The description of Haddon Hall, to which this back reference is made, runs as follows :—

"The passage under the music gallery, which serves as a through-passage to the second or upper court, contains the usual doors to the kitchen and offices. The first door opens into the buttery; the middle door leads along a narrow passage into the kitchen; by the side of the kitchen are the scullery and larders, and beyond them the bakehouse with its large fireplace and ovens; this has a separate entrance from the upper court, and has no communication with the kitchen. The third doorway leads into the pantry."

We have only to compare these arrangements of the old manor-house, as generally adopted in the colleges at Cambridge, with Bishop Neile's inventory of this portion of Auckland Castle (1628), and the case is complete.

"IN THE HALL.—*In primis*, four long tables and a short table, and eight joyned formes. Item, both sides of the hall newe wainscotted and seated.

"IN THE OLDE PANTRY.—Item, two great bings and one table, and a locke and a keye to the doore.

"IN THE OLDE KITCHIN.—Item, a table, a dresser-table in the surveying place without, and a lead cesterne.

"IN THE OLDE SCULLERIE.—Item, a lead for boyling beefe in, and a cubbord.

"IN THE BREW-HOUSE.—Item, a great brewlead with a copper bottom, a cowler of lead, a guyle-fatt, a masking-tubb, a sweat-worte tubb, a leaden trough, and an old bedstead, and two locks and two keyes for two doors in ye same.

"IN THE LARDER.—Item, a cupboard in the old larder.

"IN THE CHAMBER OF THE NORTH SIDE OF THE HALL. —A bedstead, the walls matted, and a locke and key for the door."

Here, then, we have in proximity to the hall a group of offices, which must have occupied a portion of what is now the north terrace and the ground now occupied by the raised terrace behind the chapel, and would probably also have extended to some distance southward, so as to form a portion of the eastern side of the principal court facing the great chamber. How these offices came to be supplanted by new counterparts in a different part of the castle (for even in Bishop Neile's inventory we read lower down of "the new kitchen, the new pastrie, the new scullery, the new pantrie, the newe ewry") I will explain presently. All these buildings have long disappeared. The principal of these, the kitchen, was demolished by Neile's immediate successor. Of the "dilapidations committed and suffered by Bishop Howson only," the record is, "the great kitchen pulled downe, which will cost to rebuild, as it was before, £300 ; the brewery vessels decayed, £7." The scullery would probably go with the kitchen. From the Parliamentary Survey, however, it would appear that some of these offices still remained ; but the order does not allow us to say with certainty whether these older offices or their later substitutes are intended, when the pantry, larder, etc., are mentioned. Whatever remained of these offices would probably be swept away when the hall was changed by Cosin into a chapel, so that they were no longer needed. At the east end of the north side of this new chapel Cosin left a vestry, which was approached from the chapel by a doorway. The traces of this doorway are still visible on the external wall. Whether this vestry was a survival from the ancient buildings, or a new erection of Cosin's own, we have no means of saying. It was swept away about a century later by Bishop Trevor.

Thus everything points to the identity of the present chapel with the original hall, and indeed the proof may be said to be overwhelming. But Leland, as we have seen, ascribed the building of the hall to Anthony Beck, whereas the architectural features point rather to an epoch half a century earlier than Beck's time. Moreover, Leland does not stand alone. Godwin and others say the same. A comparison of the passages, however, shows at once that Godwin and all later writers have borrowed directly or indirectly from Leland ; so that we have only one witness instead of many. What, then, shall we say of Leland's evidence? Beck was the most famous of the older bishops of Durham. He had been a great builder at Auckland. Leland rightly ascribes to him the erection of the great chamber, for we have confirmatory evidence of this not only in Graystanes, but also in this prelate's own accounts. What more natural, then, than that this hall, of whose builder authentic tradition recorded nothing, should be ascribed to this magnificent prelate, who had done so much for Auckland? Possibly he may have finished the work begun by one of his predecessors, just as Tunstall completed the dining-room pile, of which Ruthall had built the ground-floor room some years earlier. In this case he is not unlikely to have copied the earlier forms of his predecessor. He would also not unnaturally commemorate his part in the work, just as Tunstall has done, placing his arms not only on the upper part of the oriel which was his own building, but also on the ceiling of the lower story which was Ruthall's. A similar case of false attribution is the hall at Durham Castle. This was for a long time popularly assigned to Hatfield, though it is known now to have been erected at an earlier date. At all events, Leland's statement cannot for a moment weigh against the combined force of ancient notices and recent discovery. In the same paragraph he is guilty of a gigantic chronological blunder in assigning to this same Anthony Beck the erection of a "quadrant on the south-west side of the castell for ministers of the College." This quadrant was not built till about a century and a half after Beck's time by Booth or his

immediate predecessors. But Beck had erected the
original buildings of the college—distant a mile and a
half, or thereabouts, from the castle; and hence the
mistake of ascribing to him this much later erection.
There is no better authority than Leland for the actual
appearance of the hall, which he had seen; but on its
past history he has no more claim to a hearing than any
one else.

The notices of the old hall here come in and supplement the evidence thus obtained. The Parliamentary
Survey of dilapidations (1646) affords information respecting the doors. We learn from it that there were
two outer doors, and that one of these was a south door.
The other is described as on "the backside," *i.e.* the north
side, the front side being that which faced the great court
and the principal buildings of the castle. Mention is likewise made of the "stairfoot door, going up by the south
hall door," and the meaning of this seems to be determined
by another notice lower down which speaks of the "head
of the stair going unto the upper hall." In this case the
upper hall would be the minstrels' gallery. But I do not
feel at all sure about this interpretation, since the position
in which this second notice occurs might rather suggest
some other part of the house. The north and south doors
would be contiguous to the east wall of the hall, so that there
was a passage through on the lower level from outside.
This passage would be separated by a screen from the
main part of the hall which stood on the higher level;
and this screen probably would support the minstrels'
gallery. Here again we have exactly the same arrangement which is found in the hall of Trinity College, Cambridge—a very good typical instance. In addition to the

north and south doors there would doubtless be also a door at the west end of the chapel, by which the bishop and his friends could enter the hall without going into the outer court, just as there is at Trinity College. But I hesitate to apply to such a door the item in the Parliamentary Survey which specifies 90 feet of timber as required for "the entry door at the west end of the hall"; "being a double door," *i.e.* folding doors. I was tempted to do so at first, because this is the present mode of access to the building. But, when the building was arranged as a hall, the west end would be occupied by a dais, in the centre of which the bishop would sit, and we cannot imagine a large folding door right at his back. The access would probably be at the upper end of the hall through a small inobtrusive door, as in the example already cited more than once, the hall of Trinity College, Cambridge.

The north side of the great court was occupied by the hall, the south side by the chapel. I turn next to the buildings on the western side. The principal feature here was the great chamber, a rectangular room running north and south, so as to present its side to the court. There can be no question that the great chamber is represented by the present large drawing-room, for its history is continuous; and, though considerably altered from time to time, so that it presents few of its original features, it has undergone no such catastrophic change as the original hall or chapel.

The great chamber is said by Leland, and by later writers who copied him, to have been built by Anthony Beck. Leland is not infallible in such matters, as we have seen already; but we have no reason for questioning

THE MANOR-HOUSE OF AUCKLAND   207

his statement here. Graystanes had written more generally that he "constructed the Manor-House of Aukland into a chapel and chambers, in a most sumptuous way." Nothing about the place would more fully justify the epithet "sumptuous" than this spacious chamber. At all events, less than half a century later, in Bishop Hatfield's accounts (A.D. 1349-50), we find entries for some work connected with the repair of the roof of the great chamber. Nor is there anything in the extant building which throws any doubt on this date. Raine says truly of the pillars in the kitchen beneath which support the floor, that they "appear to belong to the early part of the fourteenth century." At a later date (A.D. 1513-14), under Ruthall, an item occurs for "glassing of the Great Chamber for 3 lyghts," and again another for "glassing of 3 wyndeis at the Great Chamber doyr."

Soon after this date, unless I am mistaken, an alteration was made which materially altered the character of the building, more especially its eastern aspect which looked upon the principal court. The following are my reasons for this statement:—

(1) Chambre records, of Bishop Tunstall (A.D. 1529-58), that he "construxit a fundo porticum valde speciosam et capellam ei annexam opere cæmentario in castro Dunelmensi," and again, "Construxit quoque porticum apud Auckland ; ubi etiam cubiculi in quo prandetur summitatem magnae fenestrae perfecit per Thomam Ruthall quondam episcopum prius incoeptam, aliasque reparationes circa domum praedictam fecit." On this Raine remarks (p. 64) that " In Chambre's account of Bishop Tunstall's additions to his house of Auckland

there appears to be some confusion. I infer from it, however, that he built the porch (or gallery), 'in which there are bed-chambers,' and that he finished the upper part of the great window of the dining-room, which had been begun by Bishop Ruthall"; and, he adds in a note, "In the same chapter, Chambre calls the long gallery which Tunstall constructed in Durham a *porch*." At a later point also he speaks of it as "certain" that the long gallery, commonly called Scotland, which stretches from east to west, "was built by Bishop Tunstall," referring back to the quotation of Chambre on p. 64, and adding that "the architectural remains confirm the statement."

I will say nothing about the architectural remains at present; but he has certainly misinterpreted Chambre. He seems, if I understand him, to have translated "cubiculi" as if "cubicula," and to have supposed a lacuna before "in quo prandetur." But unquestionably Dugdale has rightly interpreted Chambre, when he writes of Tunstall, "He likewise built a noble porch at Aukland, and finished the great window in the dining-room there, which was begun by Bishop Ruthall before mentioned." This becomes certain, if we compare Chambre's account of Ruthall s work, of which Tunstall's was a completion. "Hic totum," he writes, "a fundo Aucklandiae cubiculum, in quo prandetur, erexit." "Cubiculum" may be a strange word to use of the great dining-room at Auckland, considering its spaciousness and its use; but at all events, Chambre in both passages so designates it. The "porticus," therefore, has nothing whatever to do with the "cubiculi," but describes a separate work of Tunstall. "Porticus," however, cannot

THE MANOR-HOUSE OF AUCKLAND 209

be a gallery pure and simple like "Scotland." The gallery at Durham Castle is strictly a "porticus," for it leads into the great hall of Pudsey through the fine Norman doorway. This Norman doorway originally led to the open air and to a flight of steps descending into the court below. But Tunstall enclosed it, erecting a gallery or a covered portico on the same level, and making the approaches by flights of stairs at either end of the gallery.

I suppose that Beck's great chamber at Auckland was constructed somewhat like Pudsey's great chamber at Durham: that it had a great doorway in the middle of the east side facing the court; and that the descent was by a flight of steps in the same way. I believe also that Tunstall treated it in much the same way as he had treated the great chamber at Durham. This hypothesis will satisfy Chambre's language.

(2) Nor is evidence wanting of the existence of such a gallery. In Tunstall's accounts (A.D. 1543-44) there is a charge for "maykyng uppe the wall in the north ende of the gallere"; so that the gallery must have run north and south, and the notice cannot apply to "Scotland." The same seems to be the natural inference from an earlier item in these same accounts, a charge for "making trellesses for the west syde of the gallere wyndows," though here there may be some doubt. I suppose also that "the crosse gallere" mentioned elsewhere in these accounts must be this porch-gallery. The distinctive name for "Scotland" is the "Long Gallerye," as we find it designated in Bishop Neile's inventory (A.D. 1628), the "south side" being mentioned here in the context—an expression only appropriate in a structure running east

and west. Whenever "the gallery" is mentioned without any distinguishing epithet, it may be doubtful which of the two is meant, though probably in later times "Scotland" would be intended as the more prominent and distinct gallery of the two.

(3) In the drawing of Longstaffe made at the Restoration this gallery or corridor or porch in front of the great chamber is indicated. The lower part of the drawing, which was originally attached to the upper by wafers, has disappeared. On the lower margin of the remaining upper part, and beneath the windows of the great chamber, is a row of black notches, which are evidently intended to represent battlements. Any one who will compare this drawing with a picture or photograph of the front of Durham Castle, comprising Tunstall's portico, must be struck with the resemblance of the two. If I mistake not, these are the battlements of Tunstall's gallery, which has disappeared with the lower part of the drawing.

(4) But how comes it that no traces of this gallery remain in the present building? I believe that I can answer this question. Among Cosin's directions for the repairing and altering of the castle, when he came into possession of the see, is an order to John Longstaffe, dated 3rd March 1663, "to take away the old buildings before the Great Chamber or Hall." This notice perplexed me greatly, as I could not imagine to what buildings it could refer, until I saw Longstaffe's drawing, and the analogy of Durham Castle flashed upon me. Tunstall's gallery was apparently dilapidated, possibly it had been partially destroyed by Sir Arthur Haselrigg, and Cosin therefore orders its removal.

The New Building of Haselrigg

The Parliamentary Commission for taking the survey of the manor of Auckland was issued on 18th January 1646-47 A.D. The survey itself began on 22nd March of the same year, and the report was delivered on 15th April 1647 A.D. Soon after this the house and estate were sold to Sir Arthur Haselrigg, the Parliamentary general, who had commanded in the northern counties during the Civil War, and was governor of Newcastle from 30th December 1647.

Dugdale's account of what followed, so far as we are able to test it, seems to be strictly accurate. Sir A. Haselrigg was dissatisfied with the old-fashioned and inconvenient, though spacious, residence of the bishops. It could have no antiquarian or religious interest for him. He therefore designed to build "a new structure of a most noble and beautiful fabrick, all of one pile," and he took as his model the house recently erected by Oliver St. John at Thorpe in Northamptonshire.

Of Haselrigg's treatment of the older building Cosin uses very exaggerated language. He describes the manor-house or castle as having been "of late ruined and almost utterly destroyed by the ravenous sacrilege of Sir Arthur Haselrig." He elsewhere speaks of himself as "repairing and rebuilding the Castle of Aukland, which was pul'd downe and ruined by Sir Arthur Haselrig." Elsewhere, again, he states that "the usurpers, Sir A. Haselrig and others had ruin'd" his two castles of Durham and Auckland. This language is quite inconsistent with the evidence. All the chief members of the existing fabric (with the exception of the south wing built by Bishop Trevor) date from times prior to the Commonwealth. Longstaffe's drawing and Cosin's own papers confirm, if any confirmation were needed, the conviction which an examination of the actual building forces upon us. Cosin was a most munificent prelate, and he acted right nobly by the Episcopal residences of Durham and Auckland ; but he was little disposed to allow his light to be hidden under a bushel. Cosin did very much repairing and remodelling, but little or nothing which can strictly be called rebuilding. The man who caused to be inscribed on his tombstone, IN · NON · MORITVRAM · MEMORIAM · IOHANNIS · COSINI, could have had no scruple in parading his own achievements ; and this spirit of vaunting led him to exaggerate the destructiveness of others. On the other hand, Sir W. Dugdale restricts himself to the statement that Sir A. Haselrigg pulled down the "most magnificent and large Chapel," and says nothing about the demolition of any other portion of the castle. Haselrigg's object, he tells us, was to provide materials for his new buildings, and accordingly he used the stones of the demolished chapel, so far as they would go. This statement is entirely consonant with known facts. There is no evidence at all that Haselrigg pulled down any other part of the castle, but the chapel he certainly did destroy. Very probably also he would pull down any chambers attached to the chapel, or any buildings whose demolition was required to clear the area. It was perhaps at this crisis that Skirlaw's "stately gate-house" disappeared, for we hear nothing of it during Cosin's restorations.

But what was the position of this new mansion which Haselrigg thus commenced ? Raine says of it (p. 107 n.)

that "it appears to have stood on the ground stretching southwards from the east end of the chapel, with its front facing westwards towards the present great drawing-room, so as to form the third side of a quadrangle." There is nothing in the agreement—dated 1st September 1664, where "the mason is empowered to take downe from the new building soe much of the rustic ashler, etc., as shall be employed to build a wall of forty-five yards in length, running from the east end of the chapel, and facing the great chamber"—to suggest, as Raine supposes, that the wall extended over the site of the new buildings, but just the contrary. The materials for erecting this wall were taken from Sir A. Haselrigg's building, but transported to another place. The true position is roughly determined by two considerations: (1) In Longstaffe's drawing the actual site of the new building has disappeared with the loss of the lower sheet; but the name attached to the site remains at the lower margin of the extant (upper) sheet. From the position of this name we infer that the buildings must have occupied the south rather than the east side of the court, thus confronting the new chapel, not the great chamber, and that it must have been built (partially at least) on the site of the old chapel. It would not, however, be built with the view to its forming a side of the court, inasmuch as it was intended to be, as we are told, all of one pile, *i.e.* a complete block of buildings in itself, like its prototype, the mansion at Thorpe. (2) This position is confirmed by a provision in an agreement (afterwards rescinded) that the mason Longstaffe "shall remove the corner and bringe it to a square at the north-east end of the new buildinge lately begun to be erected by Sir

Arthur Heselridge." What this "corner" was, and whether it belonged to the new buildings or the old, it is impossible to say; but, in any case, the direction that this part of the new buildings should be "brought to a square," seems to show that it was a prominent feature in the great court, and being such, must be brought into harmonious relation with the other sides of the court, Cosin not having yet determined to pull down Sir A. Haselrigg's new mansion. If the site of this mansion had been where Raine places it, the north-east corner would have been the most remote and least visible from the older buildings of the castle. Moreover, direction is given in this same document that the work shall be rustic ashler "on the north side from the foundation to the top, and also part of the east side," whereas "the remainder of the east side" is to be "plain ashler, and like the plain ashler work already built there." In other words, he will have the more ornamental and elaborate treatment where it can be seen from the court. The side of the chapel towards the court is also rustic ashler from foundation to top; and Cosin will have the new building which stands face to face with it, of corresponding masonry.

The architectural character of the building would probably not be very different from that of the existing gate-house, which was an old mansion built about the same date. Of the arrangement and general features we can form some idea from the fact, which Dugdale mentions, that its model was Thorpe near Peterborough —a manor-house still in existence. Of the mullions of the windows specimens are preserved in the existing Auckland Castle; for Cosin in an extant covenant stipulates that

THE MANOR-HOUSE OF AUCKLAND 215

the mason shall transfer three windows, and three only (one with three lights, and two with two lights), and insert them in the castle in certain rooms which he specifies. These three windows are still visible; their mullions are different from those of all the other windows, and their character shows that they belong to the Parliamentary period. The three-lighted window is in the present housekeeper's room.

It is clear that Haselrigg's building was not far advanced when Cosin came into possession. In a covenant, which I have already quoted, bearing the date 2nd January 1663 (*i.e.* 1664), it is spoken of as "the new building lately begun to be erected." As more than three years and a half had elapsed since the Restoration when these words were written, Haselrigg cannot have had much time for building before he was dispossessed. He himself died in January 1660 (*i.e.* 1661). The same inference may be drawn likewise from another passage in this same covenant, where Cosin's directions for the completion seem to show that in some parts not even the shell of the building had been erected.

Dugdale states that Cosin, "soon after his consecration," observing that the new buildings were largely built of the materials taken from the "Consecrated Chapel" which he had demolished, "refused to make use of it," and that accordingly it was pulled down. He doubtless correctly describes Cosin's motive, which he may have heard from Cosin himself on the spot. But this compunction was an afterthought. Cosin's first intention had been to finish and utilize the new building. An agreement was drawn up with Longstaffe, the mason, for its completion. This was dated, as we have seen, 2nd January

1664; and a stipulation was inserted for the accomplishment of the work before Whitsuntide next ensuing. Thus Dugdale's "soon after" must be interpreted liberally, for more than three years had elapsed since his consecration (2nd December 1660). But not long after this agreement was drawn up, the misgiving seems to have seized Cosin. The covenant accordingly was cancelled. It is endorsed as "voyded," and is not so much as mentioned by Raine, though full of interesting material for his purpose. Two months later, on 3rd March, we find another agreement which breathes a different spirit. Here Longstaffe undertakes, among other provisions, to "take away the aishler in Sir Arthur Heselridg's building and remove it." This was the beginning of the end. The decisive step was the demolition of the new building. In a later document, dated 1st September 1666, portions of the stone work are to be employed for building certain walls in the court; three windows are to be transferred, as we have seen, to different parts of the old castle; and generally Longstaffe is "to have liberty to take old stone out of Sir A. Haselrigg's buildings" for use elsewhere. Lastly, at a subsequent point in this same document a sum is stipulated to be paid to him for the "takeing downe and laying safely and hansomely by, the remaineing of all the rustick ashler work, coyre-stones, doores and windows of Sir Arthur Haselrigg's building, which shall not be used in the worke before specified." At a subsequent date (29th May 1665) directions are given to remove "the frontespeece of the dore of Sir Arthur Haselrigg's building," and set it "in the middle of the wall now before the orchard," so as to form an entrance to the court of the castle; and accordingly it so appears in Buck's print.

Finally, an item appears in the accounts for October of this same year (1665) for payment to eight men, "most of them 7 days a peece," for "removing rubbish from Sir Arthur Haselrigg's new building." Thus the last remnants of the offensive building are swept away, and Cosin breathes freely.

The Two Towers

A prominent feature in the grouping of the pile must have been at one time its towers. A tower (*turellus*) is mentioned in Richard de Bury's accounts (A.D. 1337-38); and the plural "towers" appears during the episcopate of Booth (A.D. 1474-75), when there is an item for "repairing the towers." Of the two towers, of which we have explicit notice, nothing now remains. Yet they survived the troubles of the Civil War, and are mentioned by Cosin in his directions for the repair and reconstruction of the castle after the Restoration. In an agreement with Longstaffe, the mason, dated 1st September 1664, Cosin stipulates that he shall "take downe the old white wall and brick chimneyes between the old chappell tower and the staircase tower over the drawing-roome leads."

The last mentioned and less important of the two—the *staircase tower*—is easily dealt with. It was the prolongation of the existing stone staircase which leads on to the roof at the north-west corner of the great dining-room, but from a landing at a higher level than the floor of this room. It is a prominent object in Buck's print (A.D. 1728), where it appears as a tall square tower, with the clock-faces just beneath the battlements, and a lantern rising on the top of the masonry. The clock seems to have occupied this position from the earliest time when the castle possessed a clock; for in Booth's accounts (A.D. 1474-75), already referred to, we find payments made "To John Robson, carpenter, for making a new staircase to the clock; to the said John for repairing the towers; for making wheels for the bells; for making holes through the vault for the bell-ropes; for repairing the dove-cote," etc. At all events, the clock must have been in this tower from Bishop Cosin's time onwards, until the new gateway was built by Bishop Trevor in A.D. 1762. The existing clock over Trevor's gateway bears an inscription to the effect that it was *repaired* in 1760, so that it must have been transferred from some other part of the castle, and we can hardly be wrong in assuming that this staircase tower was the older home from which it then migrated. In this same tower also, in the lanthorn which crowned the masonry, was placed the bell, at least from Bishop Cosin's time, for in the same agreement, which I have quoted above, a certain payment is pledged to John Longstaffe for "hanging the bell in the staire-case towre mentioned also in the 3rd article, with long loope-lights on the four sides to let out the sound of the bell, and making a passage for the rope to the ground." The loope-lights appear in this lantern of Buck's drawing, but it is represented as hexagonal, not as quadrangular; and, if the drawing is correct, Cosin's belfry would seem to have been replaced by a late structure meanwhile. In such respects, however, no reliance can be placed on Buck's drawing, of which the perspective is very bad. "The bells" mentioned in connexion with "the towers" in Booth's accounts, as quoted above, must be sought elsewhere. Of these bells I shall have something to say in connexion with the college. The bell of the staircase tower, like the clock, has been removed to Trevor's gateway. I do not know when the tower was pulled down; but it would cease to have any use when it lost both the clock and the bell under Trevor, and its demolition may have been connected with Barrington's alterations in the roof of the great drawing-room some thirty years later.

The history of the "*old chapel tower*" presents greater difficulty. The epithet, it should be premised, belongs to "chapel," not to "tower," as Cosin speaks of the "old chapel," in contradistinction to the "new chapel," which he had constructed out of the old hall. This "chapel tower" is mentioned in the Parliamentary Survey (A.D. 1647).

For the Top of the High Tower above the stairs, and the High Chaple wanting 576 feet of stone for embattlements at 8d. per foot	£19 4 0
For the workmanship on the Timber for the roof	6 13 4
For lead for the said Tower 12 yards	6 10 0

The chapel, as we have seen, was demolished a few years later, during Sir Arthur Haselrigg's occupation; but the tower had been left standing. This appears from Cosin's covenants with Longstaffe. In the document of 2nd January 1664—the cancelled agreement to which I have referred more than once—permission is given to this mason "to take away any old stones about the Castle," after which Cosin inserts in his own hand, "or the top of the high tower there," that he might use them as building materials for repairs and reconstructions. Though this particular covenant was voided, the demolition of this tower for the sake of the materials seems to have been determined upon. It is only mentioned once again in the September of the same year—in the passage quoted above—and then only to indicate a line of direction. No traces of it remain.

As, however, it survived Haselrigg's "ravinous sacrilege," we should expect to find some indication of it in Longstaffe's drawing. This is the case.

*   *   *   *   *   *

DONNE, THE POET-PREACHER

"Tell me which of them will love him most."—ST. LUKE vii. 42.
"There are last which shall be first."—ST. LUKE xiii. 30.

DONNE's monument in St. Paul's—Its character and history an emblem of the man—His early life—His friendships—Donne as a poet—The double dislocation in his life—His conversion from Romanism—His earlier immorality and later penitence—Comparison with St. Augustine—Effects on his preaching—The secret of his power as a preacher—His reluctance to enter Holy Orders and ultimate ordination—His energy and reputation as a preacher—His extant sermons—Dean Milman's opinion—Animation of his preaching—Examples of his style—Appearance and manner of the preacher—Walton's description of him—His faults—Affectation overcome by the theme—His practical sense—His pointed sayings—His irony—The last sermon—His death—Lesson of his life and teaching.

AGAINST the wall of the south choir aisle in the Cathedral of St. Paul is a monument which very few of the thousands who visit the church daily observe, or have an opportunity of observing, but which, once seen, is not easily forgotten. It is the long, gaunt, upright figure of a man, wrapped close in a shroud, which is knotted at the head and feet, and leaves only the face exposed—a face wan, worn, almost ghastly, with the eyes closed as in death. This figure is executed in white marble, and stands on an urn of the same, as if it had just arisen therefrom. The whole is placed in a black niche, which, by its contrast, enhances the death-like paleness of the shrouded figure. Above the canopy is an inscription recording that the man whose effigy stands beneath, though his ashes are mingled with western dust, looks towards Him whose name is the Orient.[1]

This monumental figure is not less remarkable in its history than in its aspect. It is the sole memorial which has survived from the ancient church of St. Paul destroyed by the great fire. For many generations it lay neglected in the crypt, amidst mutilated fragments of other less fortunate monuments of the past, till, three or four years ago, it was rescued from its gloomy abode underground and erected in its present position, corresponding, as nearly as circumstances allowed, to the place which it occupied in the old Cathedral before the fire.[2] The canopy and inscription were restored from an ancient engraving. In its history and in its character alike this monument is a fit emblem of him whom it figures; for it speaks of a death, a resurrection, a saving as by fire.

[1] An allusion to the Vulgate rendering of Zech. vi. 12, "Ecce vir Oriens nomen ejus" (comp. iii. 8), translated "The man whose name is the Branch" in the Authorised Version. This text is quoted several times in Donne's *Sermons*, and appears to have been a favourite with him.

[2] In old St. Paul's it stood against a pier so as to face eastward, the aspect being adapted to the words; but this position was impossible in the present Cathedral, unless the monument had been placed in some other part of the building.

DONNE, THE POET-PREACHER

It is the effigy of John Donne, who was Dean of St. Paul's shortly before the outbreak of the Great Rebellion.

Moreover, it has a peculiar interest arising from the circumstances under which it was erected in the first instance. It was not such a memorial as Donne's surviving friends might think suitable to commemorate the deceased, but it was the very monument which Donne himself designed as a true emblem of his past life and his future hopes. His friend and biographer relates[1] that, being urged to give directions for his monument, he caused an urn to be carved; that he wrapped himself in a winding sheet, and stood thereupon "with his eyes shut and with so much of the sheet turned aside as might show his lean, pale, and death-like face, which was purposely turned towards the East, from whence he expected the second coming of his and our Saviour Jesus"; that, in this posture, he had a picture of himself taken, which "he caused to be set by his bedside, where it continued, and became his hourly object till his death"; and that from this picture the sculpture was executed after his decease, the inscription having been written by Donne himself. In its quaint affectation and in its appalling earnestness this monument recalls the very mind of the man himself.

John Donne was born in 1573, the year after the

[1] Walton's *Life of Donne*, p. 131. The edition quoted is that published by Causton, "with some original notes by an Antiquary."

Massacre of St. Bartholomew. He was the child of Roman Catholic parents, and in their faith he was brought up. At the age of eleven he went to Hart Hall, Oxford; at the age of fourteen or thereabouts he was "transplanted" to Trinity College, Cambridge. At neither University did he proceed to a degree, for his friends had a conscientious objection to his taking the required oath. He was still only in his seventeenth year when he commenced the study of the law, and soon after he entered Lincoln's Inn. Of his subsequent life for some years we catch only glimpses here and there. He was a courtier and an associate of nobles and statesmen. He numbered among his friends and acquaintances nearly all the most famous literary men of the day — Ben Jonson, Francis Bacon, Sir Henry Wotton, Selden, Bishop Hall, Bishop Montague, Bishop Andrewes, George Herbert, Izaak Walton. He was a great traveller and a great linguist, a diligent student, a man of wide and varied accomplishments. His versatility is a constant theme of admiration with those who knew him.[1] At the age of twenty he wrote poems which his contemporaries regarded as masterpieces. His fame as a poet was greater in his own age than it has ever been since. During the last century, which had no toleration for subtle conceits and rugged rhythms,

---

[1] See Grosart's preface to Donne's *Poems*, ii. p. xvi. *sq.* Coleridge also, comparing him with Shakespeare, speaks of his "lordliness of opulence," *ib.* p. xxxviii.

it was unduly depreciated; but now again it has emerged from its eclipse. No quaintness of conception and no recklessness of style and no harshness of metre can hide the true poetic genius which flashes out from his nobler pieces.

It has been said that God's heroes are made out of broken lives. There is indeed vouchsafed to the steady progressive growth of a career which has known no abrupt transition, and in which the days are "bound each to each by natural piety," a calm wisdom, a clear insight, an impressive influence, unattainable on any other terms; but for the fire, the passion, the impulsive energy which bears down all opposition, we must not uncommonly look to a dislocated life. This dislocation may be either of two kinds. It may be a dislocation of theological belief, like Luther's, or it may be a dislocation of moral character, like Ignatius Loyola's and John Bunyan's; the dislocation of the convert or the dislocation of the penitent. Donne's, like Augustine's, was both the one and the other.

He grew up to maturity, as we saw, a Roman Catholic; but while still a young man he began to study the Roman controversy, as he himself says, "with no inordinate haste nor precipitation in binding myself to any local religion." "I had a larger work to do," he writes, "than many other men." He tells us that in this investigation he "surveyed and digested the whole body of divinity" relating to the controversy; and he calls God to witness, that he "proceeded therein with humility and diffidence in himself," and with "frequent prayer and equal and indifferent affections."[1] As the result of this search after truth, he joined the Anglican communion. It seems to me that the influence of this change has impressed itself, as it could hardly fail to do, on his preaching. In saying this, I do not refer to the purely controversial parts, where the fact must be obvious. The remark applies to the general scope and character of his sermons. They owe their chief force to the intense earnestness with which he dwells on the atoning power of Christ's passion; and I cannot doubt that, from the intellectual side, his vividness and grasp of conception on this point owed much to his study of the Roman controversy.

Of the other dislocation, the discontinuity of his moral life, it is more painful to speak; but no study of Donne as a preacher would be at all adequate which failed to take account of this fact. His friend Izaak Walton, in an elegy written a few days after his death, has incidentally compared him to the chief penitent in the Gospel. Contrasting with the light effusions of his earlier years the religious poems which he assigns to a later period, he asks—

> "Did his rich soul conceive
> And in harmonious, holy numbers weave
> A crown of sacred sonnets, fit to adorn
> A dying martyr's brow, or to be worn

---

[1] Preface to his *Pseudo-Martyr*, p. 3.

> On that blest head of Mary Magdalen
> After she wiped Christ's feet, but not till then ?
> Did he—fit for such penitents as she
> And he to use—leave us a Litany
> Which all devout men love ?"[1]

Of the fact I fear there can be little doubt that at one time he had led an immoral life. It is indeed most unjust to measure the self-accusations of the devout servant of God by the common standard of human language. The holiest men are the most exacting with themselves. Bitter cries of anguish— almost of despair—will be wrung from the saint for sins which would cost the worldling not one moment of sleeplessness and not one prick of remorse. Therefore, if they had stood alone, we ought not to have laid too great stress on those "tones of pain, thrills of contrition, stingings of accusation, wails over abiding stains and wounds, and passionate weeping," which, in the language of a recent writer,[2] are discernible in Donne's letters and sermons. But unhappily his shame is written across his extant poems in letters of fire. In some of these there are profligacies which it were vain to excuse as purely imaginative efforts of the poet, or unworthy condescensions to the base tastes of the age. We are driven to the conclusion that they reflect—at least to some extent—the sensuality of the man himself. Of such an offence I can offer no palliation. I know

[1] *Life*, p. 154.
[2] Grosart, Preface to Donne's *Poems*, vol. ii. p. xvii.

no crime more unpardonable in itself, or more fatal in its consequences, than this of prostituting the highest gifts of genius to a propaganda of vice and shame, this of poisoning the wells of a nation's literature and spreading moral death through generations yet unborn.[1] Donne's penitence was intense; he did all he could to retrieve the consequences of his sin. But he could not undo his work, could not blot out the printed page. "In his penitential years," says his biographer, "viewing some of those pieces that had been loosely—God knows, too loosely—scattered in his youth, he wished that they had been abortive, or so short-lived that his own eyes had witnessed their funerals."[2]

But whatever may have been the sins of his youth and early manhood, his married life shows him a changed man. His clandestine union brought him only sorrows and trials from a worldly point of view; but he was an affectionate and true husband, faithful to his wife during her lifetime, and loyal to her memory in a solitary widowhood of many years after her death.

The comparison of Donne with the great African father was too obvious to escape notice. It is touched upon by his earliest critic, his contemporary and biographer;[3] and it is drawn out by one of his

[1] It must be remembered, however, that Donne was not in many cases responsible for the *publication* of his poems. They were published for the most part after his death.

[2] P. 106 *sq.* The sentence is somewhat differently worded in different editions.

[3] P. 65 *sq.*

latest. Of one of his religious poems the present Archbishop of Dublin writes : " It is the genuine cry of one engaged in that most terrible of all struggles, wherein, as we are winners or losers, we have won all or lost all." Then, adverting to this parallel, he adds : " There was in Donne the same tumultuous youth, the same entanglement in youthful lusts, the same conflict with these, and the same final deliverance from them ; and then the same passionate and personal grasp of the central truths of Christianity, linking itself, as this did, with all that he had suffered and all that he had sinned, and all through which, by God's grace, he had victoriously struggled."[1] It is no marvel, then, to find Donne himself quoting St. Augustine more frequently than any of the fathers—this " sensible and blessed father," this " tender blessed father," as he affectionately calls him.

The bearing of these facts on his preaching will be evident. This moral experience was the complement of his intellectual experience. It taught him to feel and to absorb into himself, as the other taught him to understand and to reason about, the doctrine of Christ's atoning grace. What penitence, what tears, what merits of his own *could* wash out the stains with which such a life as his was imbrued ? It was therefore no pious platitude, no barren truism, no phrase of conventional orthodoxy, but the pro-

---

[1] *Household Book of English Poetry*, p. 404, quoted by Grosart, Donne's *Poems*, vol. ii. p. xviii.

found conviction of a sinful, sorrowing, forgiven, thanksgiving man, when he speaks of "the sovereign balm of our souls, the blood of Christ Jesus."[1] Hear now these lines, which he wrote in his later years on a sick-bed, and which often after, when "sung to the organ by the choristers of St. Paul's," as he himself told a friend, "raised the affections of his heart and quickened his graces of zeal and gratitude."[2]

> " Wilt thou forgive that sin, through which I run,
>   And do run still, though still I do deplore ?
> When Thou hast done, Thou hast not done ;
>   For I have more.
>
> " Wilt Thou forgive that sin which I have won
>   Others to sin, and made my sin their door ?
> Wilt Thou forgive that sin which I did shun
>   A year or two, but wallowed in a score ?
> When Thou hast done, Thou hast not done ;
>   For I have more.
>
> " I have a sin of fear, that when I've spun
>   My last thread, I shall perish on the shore ;
> But swear by Thyself, that at my death Thy Son
>   Shall shine, as He shines now and heretofore ;
> And having done that Thou hast done ;
>   I fear no more."[3]

"Simon, I have somewhat to say unto thee . . . Tell me which of them will love him most ? Simon

---

[1] Donne's *Works*, vol. i. p. 53, ed. Alford. The references to the sermons below are taken from this edition, but I have collated the quotations, where I had the opportunity, with the original editions.

[2] Walton's *Life*, p. 111.

[3] Donne's *Poems*, vol. ii. p. 341 *sq.* (ed. Grosart).

answered and said, I suppose that he to whom he forgave most. And He said unto him, Thou hast rightly judged. . . .

"Wherefore I say unto thee, Her sins, which are many, are forgiven; for she loved much : but to whom little is forgiven, the same loveth little."[1]

Of Donne's romantic career it has been said that his life is more poetical than his poetry.[2] We might, without exaggeration, adapt this epigram to his preaching, and say that his life was a sermon more eloquent than all his sermons.

If, then, I were asked to describe in few words the secret of his power as a preacher, I should say that it was the contrition and the thanksgiving of the penitent acting upon the sensibility of the poet.[3]

Donne remained a layman till his forty-second year. He was pressed again and again by friends who knew his gifts to enter Holy Orders, but for some years he hesitated. His hesitation was due partly to an unwillingness to incur the suspicion with his own conscience of being influenced by motives of self-interest, but still more by the recollection of his past life. He himself had long repented of the sins of his youth, and "banished them his affections";

[1] St. Luke, vii. 40-47.
[2] Campbell, as represented by Milman, *Annals of St. Paul's Cathedral*, p. 324 ; but Campbell himself, if I have found the right reference, makes the very commonplace remark that "the life of Donne is more interesting than his poetry" (*British Poets*, vol. iii. p. 73).
[3] Donne seems to have the best right to the title of the poet-preacher, a designation which has sometimes been given to another.

but though forgiven by God, they were not forgotten by men; and he feared that they might bring some censure on himself, or worse, some dishonour on his sacred calling, if he complied.[1]

At length he yielded, after much delay, to the repeated solicitations of the king himself. In the year 1614 he was ordained; and seven years afterwards he was promoted to the Deanery of St. Paul's, which he held till his death. He died in the fifty-ninth year of his age, having been sixteen years in orders.

As a layman he had been notably a poet; as a clergyman he was before all things a preacher. He had remarkable gifts as an orator, and he used them well. Henceforward preaching was the main business of his life. After he had preached a sermon, "he never gave his eyes rest," we are told, "till he had chosen out a new text, and that night cast his sermon into a form, and his text into divisions, and the next day he took himself to consult the fathers, and so commit his meditations to his memory, which was excellent."[2] On the Saturday he gave himself an entire holiday, so as to refresh body and mind, "that he might be enabled to do the work of the day following not faintly, but with courage and cheerfulness." When first ordained he shunned preaching before town congregations. He would retire to some country church with a single friend, and so try his wings. His first sermon was preached

[1] Walton's *Life*, p. 41.   [2] *Ibid.* p. 119.

in the quiet village of Paddington. But his fame grew rapidly; and he soon took his rank as the most powerful preacher of his day in the English Church. Others envied him and murmured, says an admirer, that, having been called to the vineyard late in the day, he received his penny with the first.[1]

More than a hundred and fifty of his sermons are published. Some of them were preached at Lincoln's Inn, where he held the Lectureship; others at St. Dunstan's-in-the-West, of which church he was vicar; others at Whitehall, in his turn as Royal Chaplain, or before the Court on special occasions; others, and these the most numerous, at St. Paul's. Of this last class a few were delivered at the Cross, by special appointment, but the majority within the Cathedral, when year after year, according to the rule which is still in force at St. Paul's, he preached as Dean at the great festivals of the Church—Christmas and Easter and Whitsunday—or when he expounded the Psalms assigned to his prebendal stall, or on various incidental occasions.

An eminent successor of Donne, the late Dean Milman, finds it difficult to "imagine, when he surveys the massy folios of Donne's sermons—each sermon spreads out over many pages—a vast congregation in the Cathedral or at Paul's Cross listening not only with patience, but with absorbed interest,

[1] Elegy by Mr. R. B., attached to *Poems* by John Donne (1669), p. 393.

with unflagging attention, even with delight and rapture, to those interminable disquisitions. . . ." "It is astonishing to us," he adds, "that he should hold a London congregation enthralled, unwearied, unsatiated."[1]

And yet I do not think that the secret of his domination is far to seek.

> "Fervet immensusque ruit."

There is throughout an energy, a glow, an impetuosity, a force as of a torrent, which must have swept his hearers onward despite themselves. This rapidity of movement is his characteristic feature. There are faults in abundance, but there is no flagging from beginning to end. Even the least manageable subjects yield to his untiring energy. Thus he occupies himself largely with the minute interpretation of scriptural passages. This exegesis is very difficult of treatment before a large and miscellaneous congregation. But with Donne it is always interesting. It may be subtle, wire-drawn, fanciful at times, but it is keen, eager, lively, never pedantic or dull. So, again, his sermons abound in quotations from the fathers; and this burden of patristic reference would have crushed any common man. But here the quotations are epigrammatic in themselves; they are tersely rendered, they are vigorously applied, and the reader is never wearied by them. Donne is, I think, the most animated of the great Anglican preachers.

[1] *Annals of St. Paul's Cathedral*, p. 328.

I select two or three examples out of hundreds which might be chosen, as exhibiting this eagerness of style, lit up by the genius of a poet, and heated by the zeal of an evangelist. Hear this, for instance :—

"God's house is the house of prayer. It is His court of requests. There he receives petitions; there He gives orders upon them. And you come to God in His house as though you came to keep Him company, to sit down and talk with Him half an hour; or you come as ambassadors, covered in His presence, as though ye came from as great a prince as He. You meet below, and there make your bargains for biting, for devouring usury, and then you come up hither to prayers, and so make God your broker. You rob and spoil and eat His people as bread by extortion and bribery, and deceitful weights and measures, and deluding oaths in buying and selling, and then come hither, and so make God your receiver, and His house a den of thieves. . . . As if the Son of God were but the son of some lord that had been your schoolfellow in your youth, and so you continue a boldness to him ever after; so because you have been brought up with Christ from your cradle, and catechised in His name, His name becomes less reverend unto you; and *sanctum et terribile*, holy and reverend, holy and terrible, should His name be."[1]

Or this :—

"In the earth, in the grave there is no distinction

[1] *Works*, vol. iii. p. 217 *sq.*

The angel that shall call us out of that dust will not stand to survey who lies naked, who in a coffin, who in wood, who in lead, who in a fine, who in a coarser sheet; in that one day of the resurrection there is not a forenoon for lords to rise first and an afternoon for meaner persons to rise after, Christ was not whipped to save beggars and crowned with thorns to save kings: He died, He suffered all, for all."[1]

Or hear this again, which was a favourite passage with Coleridge:—

"Death comes equally to us all and makes us all equal when it comes. The ashes of an oak in the chimney are no epitaph of that oak, to tell me how high or how large that was; it tells me not what flocks it sheltered while it stood, nor what men it hurt when it fell. The dust of great persons' graves is speechless too; it says nothing, it distinguishes nothing. As soon the dust of a wretch whom thou wouldst not, as of a prince whom thou couldst not look upon, will trouble thine eyes, if the wind blow it thither; and when a whirlwind hath blown the dust of the churchyard into the church, and the man sweeps out the dust of the church into the churchyard, who will undertake to sift those dusts again, and to pronounce, 'This is the patrician, this is the noble flour; and this is the yeomanly, this the plebeian bran'?"[2]

Or listen again to this most terrible passage of all. I do not quote it from any sympathy with this

[1] *Works*, vol. vi. p. 237.   [2] *Ibid.* vol. i. p. 241.

mode of appeal to the Christian conscience, but merely as illustrating the appalling power of the preacher when he puts out his strength.

"*It is a fearful thing to fall into the hands of the living God;* but to fall out of the hands of the living God is a horror beyond our expression, beyond our imagination.

"That God should let my soul fall out of His hand into a bottomless pit, and roll an unremovable stone upon it, and leave it to that which it finds there (and it shall find that there which it never imagined till it came thither), and never think more of that soul, never have more to do with it. That of that providence of God, that studies the life of every weed and worm and ant and spider and toad and viper, there should never, never any beam flow out upon me; that that God who looked upon me when I was nothing, and called me when I was not, as though I had been, out of the womb and depth of darkness, will not look upon me now, when, though a miserable and a banished and a damned creature, yet I am His creature still, and contribute something to His glory, even in my damnation; that that God who hath often looked upon me in my foulest uncleanness and when I had shut out the eye of the day, the sun, and the eye of the night, the taper, and the eyes of all the world, with curtains and windows and doors, did yet see me, and see me in mercy, by making me see that He saw me, and sometimes brought me to a present remorse and (for that time) to a forbearing of that sin, should so turn Himself from me to His glorious saints and angels, as that no saint nor angel nor Jesus Christ Himself should ever pray Him to look towards me, never remember Him that such a soul there is; that that God who hath so often said to my soul, *Quare morieris?* 'Why wilt thou die?' and so often sworn to my soul, *Vivit Dominus*, 'As the Lord liveth, I would not have thee die but live,' will neither let me die nor let me live, but die an everlasting life and live an everlasting death; that that God who when He could not get into me by standing and knocking, by His ordinary means of entering, by His word, His mercies, hath applied His judgments and hath shaked the house, this body, with agues and palsies, and set this house on fire with fevers and calentures, and frighted the master of the house, my soul, with horrors and heavy apprehensions, and so made an entrance into me; that that God should frustrate all His own purposes and practices upon me, and leave me and cast me away, as though I had cost Him nothing; that this God at last should let this soul go away as a smoke, as a vapour, as a bubble, and that then this soul cannot be a smoke, a vapour, nor a bubble, but must lie in darkness as long as the Lord of light is light itself, and never spark of that light reach to my soul. . . ."[1]

Listen to such words as I have read; and to

[1] *Works*, vol. iii. p. 386 *sq*.

complete the effect summon up in imagination the appearance and manner of the preacher. Recall him as he is seen in the portrait attributed to Vandyck—the keen, importuning "melting eye,"[1] the thin, worn features, the poetic cast of expression, half pensive, half gracious. Add to this the sweet tones of his voice and the "speaking action,"[2] which is described by eye-witnesses as more eloquent than the words of others, and you will cease to wonder at the thraldom in which he held his audience. "A preacher in earnest," writes Walton, "weeping sometimes *for* his auditory, sometimes *with* them; always preaching to himself; like an angel *from* a cloud but *in* none; carrying some, as St. Paul was, to heaven in holy raptures and enticing others by a sacred art and courtship to amend their lives; here picturing a vice so as to make it ugly to those who practised it, and a virtue so as to make it beloved even by those that loved it not. . . ."[3] Indeed we cannot doubt that he himself was alive to that feeling which he ascribes to the "blessed fathers" when preaching, "a holy delight to be heard and to be heard with delight."[4]

Donne's sermons are not faultless models of pulpit oratory. From this point of view they cannot be studied as the sermons of the great French preachers may be studied. Under the

[1] Walton's *Life*, p. 150.
[2] Elegy by Mr. Mayne, attached to *Poems* by John Donne (1669), p. 387.
[3] *Life*, p. 69.   [4] *Works*, vol. i. p. 98.

circumstances this was almost an impossibility. Preaching his hour's sermon once or twice weekly, he had not time to arrange and rearrange, to prune, to polish, to elaborate. As it is, we marvel at the profusion of learning, the richness of ideas and imagery, the abundance in all kinds, poured out by a preacher who thus lived, as it were, from hand to mouth.

Moreover, the taste of the age for fantastic imagery, for subtle disquisition, for affectations of language and of thought, exercised a fascination over him. Yet even here he is elevated above himself and his time by his subject. There is still far too much of that conceit of language, of that subtlety of association, of that "sport with ideas," which has been condemned in his verse compositions; but, compared with his poems, his sermons are freedom and simplicity itself. And, whenever his theme rises, he rises too; and then in the giant strength of an earnest conviction he bursts these green withes which a fantastic age has bound about him, as the thread of tow snaps at the touch of fire. Nothing can be more direct or more real than his eager impetuous eloquence, when he speaks of God, of redemption, of heaven, of the sinfulness of human sin, of the bountifulness of Divine Love.

At such moments he is quite the most modern of our older Anglican divines. He speaks directly to our time, because he speaks to all times. If it be the special aim of the preacher to convince of sin and of righteousness and of judgment, then Donne deserves to be reckoned the first of our classic preachers. We may find elsewhere more skilful arrangement, more careful oratory, more accurate exegesis, more profuse illustration; but here is the light which flashes and the fire which burns.

Donne's learning was enormous; and yet his sermons probably owe more to his knowledge of men than to his knowledge of books. The penitent is too apt to shrink into the recluse. Donne never yielded to this temptation. He himself thus rebukes the mistaken extravagance of penitence: "When men have lived long from God, they never think they come near enough to Him, except they go beyond Him."[1] No contrition was more intense than his; but he did not think to prove its reality by cutting himself off from the former interests and associations of his life. He had been a man of the world before; and he did not cease to be a man in the world now. "Beloved"—he says this term "beloved" is his favourite mode of address—"Beloved, salvation itself being so often presented to us in the names of glory and of joy, we cannot think that the way to that glory is a sordid life affected here, an obscure, a beggarly, a negligent abandoning of all ways of preferment or riches or estimation in this world, for the glory of heaven shines down in these beams hither. . . . As God loves a cheerful giver, so He loves a cheerful taker that takes hold

[1] *Works*, vol. ii. p. 31.

of His mercies and His comforts with a cheerful heart."[1] This healthy, vigorous good sense is the more admirable in Donne, because it is wedded to an intense and passionate devotion.

I wish that time would allow me to multiply examples of his lively imagination flashing out in practical maxims and lighting up the common things of life; as, for instance, where he pictures the general sense of insecurity on the death of Elizabeth: "Every one of you in the city were running up and down like ants with their eggs bigger than themselves, every man with his bags, to seek where to hide them safely."[2] Or where he enforces the necessity of watchfulness against minor temptations: "As men that rob houses thrust in a child at the window, and he opens greater doors for them, so lesser sins make way for greater."[3] Or when he describes the little effect of preaching on the heartless listener: "He hears but the logic or the rhetoric or the ethic or the poetry of the sermon, but the sermon of the sermon he hears not."[4] Of such pithy sayings Donne's sermons are an inexhaustible storehouse, in which I would gladly linger; but I must hasten on to speak of one other feature before drawing to a close. Irony is a powerful instrument in the preacher's hands, if he knows how to wield it; otherwise it were better left alone. The irony of Donne is piercing. Hear the withering scorn which he pours on those who think

[1] *Works*, vol. ii. p. 142.
[2] *Ibid.* vol. vi. p. 137.
[3] *Ibid.* vol. ii. p. 556.
[4] *Ibid.* vol. i. p. 72.

to condone sinful living by a posthumous bequest: "We hide our sins in His house by hypocrisy all our lives, and we hide them at our deaths, perchance, with an hospital. And truly we had need do so; when we have impoverished God in His children by our extortions, and wounded Him and lamed Him in them by our oppressions, we had need to provide God an hospital."[1] Or hear this again, on the criticism of sermons: "Because God calls preaching foolishness, you take God at His word and think preaching a thing under you. Hence it is that you take so much liberty in censuring and comparing preacher and preacher."[2] And lastly, observe the profound pathos and awe which are veiled under the apparent recklessness of these daring words: "At how cheap a price was Christ tumbled up and down in this world! It does almost take off our pious scorn of the low price at which Judas sold Him, to consider that His Father sold Him to the world for nothing."[3]

For preaching Donne lived; and in preaching he died. He rose from a sick-bed and came to London to take his customary sermon at Whitehall on the first Friday in Lent. Those who saw him in the pulpit, says Walton quaintly, must "have asked that question in Ezekiel, 'Do these bones live?'" The sermon was felt to be the swan's dying strain. Death was written in his wan and wasted features, and spoke through his faint and hollow voice.

[1] *Works*, vol. ii. p. 555. [2] *Ibid.* vol. ii. p. 219.
[3] *Ibid.* vol. i. p. 61.

The subject was in harmony with the circumstances. He took as his text[1] the passage in the Psalms, "Unto God the Lord belong the issues of death." His hearers said at the time that "Dr. Donne had preached his own funeral sermon."

The sermon was published. It betrays in part a diminution of his wonted fire and animation. We seem to see the preacher struggling painfully with his malady. But yet it is remarkable. The theme and the circumstances alike invest it with a peculiar solemnity; and there are flashes of the poet-preacher still.

"This whole world," he says, "is but a universal churchyard, but one common grave : and the life and motion that the greatest persons have in it is but as the shaking of buried bodies in their graves by an earthquake."[2]

"The worm is spread under thee, and the worm covers thee. *There* is the mats and carpet that lie under, and *there* is the state and the canopy that hangs over the greatest of the sons of men."[3]

"The tree lies as it falls, it is true, but yet it is not the last stroke that fells the tree, nor the last word nor the last gasp that qualifies the man."[4]

Hear now the closing words, and you will not be at a loss to conceive the profound impression which they must have left on his hearers, as the dying utterance of a dying man :—

[1] *Life*, p. 135 *sq.* [2] *Works*, vol. vi. p. 283.
[3] *Ibid.* p. 288. [4] *Ibid.* p. 290.

"There we leave you in that blessed dependency, to hang upon Him that hangs upon the Cross. There bathe in His tears, there suck at His wounds, and lie down in peace in His grave, till He vouchsafes you a resurrection and an ascension into that kingdom which He hath purchased for you with the inestimable price of His incorruptible blood. Amen."

Amen it was. He had prayed that he might die in the pulpit, or (if not this) that he might die of the pulpit; and his prayer was granted. From this sickness he never recovered; the effort hastened his dissolution; and, after lingering on a few weeks, he died on the last day of March 1631.

This study of Donne as a preacher will be fitly closed with the last stanza from his poem entitled, "Hymn to God, my God, in my sickness," which sums up the broad lesson of his life and teaching :—

"So in *His* purple wrapped, receive me, Lord ;
By these *His* thorns give me His other crown ;
And as to others' souls I preached Thy Word,
Be this my text, my sermon to mine own :
Therefore, that He may raise, the Lord throws down."[1]

---

[1] *Poems*, vol. ii. p. 340.

THE END

www.ingramcontent.com/pod-product-compliance
Lightning Source LLC
Chambersburg PA
CBHW062012220426
43662CB00010B/1301